Securing Peace
in the Middle East

Securing Peace in the Middle East

Project on
Economic Transition

Edited by

Stanley Fischer
Leonard J. Hausman
Anna D. Karasik
Thomas C. Schelling

*The Institute for Social
and Economic Policy in
the Middle East*

The MIT Press
Cambridge, Massachusetts
London, England

© 1994 Massachusetts Institute of Technology

This book was set in Palatino by The MIT Press and was printed and bound in the United States of America.

Library of Congress Cataloging-in-Publication Data

Securing peace in the Middle East: project on economic transition /
  Stanley Fischer. . . [et al.].
    p.   cm.
  Includes bibliographical references.
  ISBN 0-262-06168-6
  1. West Bank–Economic policy. 2. Gaza Strip–Economic policy. 3. Israel–Foreign economic relations–Jordan. 4. Jordan–Foreign economic relations–Israel. 5. Middle East–Economic integration. I. Fischer, Stanley.
  HC415.25.Z7W4915 1994   93-41541
  338.953'1–dc20   CIP

Contents

Foreword   vii
Joseph A. Califano, Jr.

Introduction to the MIT Press Edition   ix

Introductory Note   xiii
Leonard J. Hausman and Anna D. Karasik

Acknowledgments   xv
Stanley Fischer and Thomas C. Schelling

Editorial Board   xix

Chairs of Working Groups   xxi

Participating Economists   xxiii

Contributors   xxvii

Executive Summary   xxix

1 **Summary and Conclusions**   1

Stanley Fischer and Thomas C. Schelling,
Steering Committee Co-Chairs

2 **Agriculture, Industry, Services, and Trade**   45

Raymond Vernon, *Chair*

3 **Palestinian-Israeli-Jordanian Labor Mobility:
The Current Situation and Issues for a
Peaceful Future**   69

Richard B. Freeman, *Chair*

4 **Institutional Structure for the Palestinian Economy
During the Transition Period**   93

Henry Rosovsky, *Chair*

5 **Fiscal Management**   115

Thomas C. Schelling, *Chair*

6 **Financial and Monetary Arrangements in the
Palestinian Transition**   129

Lester C. Thurow, *Chair*

7 **The Management of Foreign Aid to the West Bank
and Gaza: Goals and Organization**   145

Dwight Perkins, *Chair*

8 **The Way Ahead**   165

Stanley Fischer, *Steering Committee Co-Chair*

Foreword

Policy planning for a new economic era in the Middle East is behind schedule. While it is impossible to predict precisely when the parties will sign an initial accord, the Middle East peace talks are in a serious stage and could yield results at any time. The question is whether the parties are prepared to move quickly from the cessation of hostilities to the normalization of economic relations. At this point, they are not prepared to establish Palestinian commercial banks; to trade goods and services; to facilitate regional tourism; and to enrich each other by the cross-border flow of technology and capital. All this takes planning, and that has not been done. Were a peace accord to be achieved soon, the parties would not be in a position to normalize economic relations.

Indeed, economic policy planning could not proceed until now: through governments, because appropriate political conditions had not been established; or through international agencies, such as the World Bank, because such organizations are constrained by their members to mirror, and not supersede, existing conflicts. Only in the voluntary sector could discussions among the parties be conducted on an unconstrained basis. The Institute for Social and Economic Policy in the Middle East recognized the vacuum, understood the opportunity, consulted

with the relevant political leaders, and identified a corps of highly qualified professional economists from the region who could
begin the planning process away from the glare of public attention.

Israelis, Jordanians, and Palestinians, as well as other interested parties, can learn from this report the central tendency in
thinking on economic policy among these three parties. All want
free trade; all want infrastructure projects that integrate and benefit the three of them simultaneously; all want to proceed cau-
tiously in changing policy on regional labor migration. As a
result of this report, therefore, the parties can reduce the time it
takes to learn each other's positions; and thus move quickly
towards binding agreements on their future economic relationships.

My colleagues and I on the Institute's board—along with our
far-flung network of Christians, Jews, and Muslims working
together for peace in the Middle East—are pleased to have supported the project that has yielded this report. May peace be our
common reward.

Joseph A. Califano, Jr.
Founding Chairman of the Board
The Institute for Social and Economic Policy
in the Middle East

Introduction to
the MIT Press Edition

Securing Peace in the Middle East was completed in June 1993. The report received widespread attention in the Middle East, Europe, and the United States when it was presented in June and July. Reactions differed. In Jordan, in the Palestinian press in Jerusalem, in the Israeli press, and in some of the Gulf states, the report was taken seriously, and its basic arguments won almost unanimous approval. Policymakers involved in the peace process in the United States likewise treated the report as a realistic and timely document. The friendly reception we received from the press in the United States and Europe was, however, mixed with polite skepticism about the relevance of a report that started from the assumption that "there would be created via a political agreement 'a Palestinian entity with economic sovereignty.'"

Two months later, at the end of August, the Israel–PLO agreement spelled out the details of precisely such an arrangement. Overnight our report lost its visionary status and became instead one of the two basic reference documents (the other is the World Bank report on the economy of the Occupied Territories) on the economics of Palestinian transition.

Typos, misspellings, and this Introduction aside, we have left the text of *Securing Peace* as it was in June. We elected not to make changes for three reasons: most important, there are no recommendations that we would change in light of developments since June; second, the text of the report had been agreed to by all participants and it would have taken time to get their agreement to changes; and third, the text and especially the prefatory material captures perfectly the mood in which the report was completed—of elation at the fact that Israelis, Jordanians, and Palestinians could cooperate successfully in thinking through practical solutions to their common problems.

To quote from the report: "To our knowledge, this is the first document ever prepared by Israelis, Jordanians, and Palestinians. . . . We hope and believe that both the report and the spirit in which it was written will contribute to the economic development of the Palestinian, Jordanian, and Israeli economies, and thus to peace." We believe that now even more firmly than in June.

With the signing of the Israel–PLO agreement, the international community, the Israelis, and the Jordanians have acquired an enormous stake in the economic success of the Palestinians. The international community jumped into action. Aid pledged at the donors' conference in Washington in early October should ensure that the Palestinians receive at least $400 million a year in aid for the first few years after the Palestinian Interim Self-Government Authority takes over. The donors are providing funding for technical assistance to help build up Palestinian institutional capacity. It appears also that the World Bank will play a key role in coordinating aid, although it remains to be seen how successful that coordination will be in reducing the pressures from competing public and private aid agencies on Palestinian economic matters. It is striking that, as stated in Chapter 7, no less than 66 aid agencies were active in the Occupied Territories in 1992.

External financial assistance is essential for the economic success of the Palestinian entity, and that component will be largely taken care of if the donors are successful in coordinating aid and in translating pledges into money. But there has been much less early movement on the even more crucial issue of the economic framework within which the Palestinian economy will operate.

The initial agreement between the PLO and Israel specifies the economic framework only in very general terms. These issues—trade, fiscal coordination and revenue recovery, monetary and financial arrangements, and labor flows—are all discussed extensively in the report that follows. We still strongly support the report's recommendations on these issues, as well as those relating to the relations among Israel, Jordan, and the Palestinians. We repeat the recommendation of Chapter 8 that Israeli, Jordanian, and Palestinian teams of experts should already be working to prepare practical recommendations in these areas, perhaps with outside assistance.

There seems to have been even less attention paid to the important regional projects that can help undergird the peace. These include projects in transportation, tourism, energy, and water. They also include the setting up of a regional bank for development and economic cooperation, which would encourage functional cooperation among the countries and peoples of the region. We are enthusiastic also about the possibility of establishing a regional policy research institute.

Our institute, ISEPME, proposes working on several of these projects during the next year, including the regional bank and research institute, and water issues. We believe an initial Israeli–Palestinian–Jordanian free-trade area will develop into a wider free-trade area, and we intend to work out possible ways of making that happen. Down the road are the important and delicate issues of the return of refugees, and of the future of Israeli settlements in the Palestinian entity. Precisely because these issues are politically difficult, we believe that a private sector institution like ours can make an important contribution to thinking about and solving them.

Important as these issues are for the longer term, the short-term imperative is for the Palestinian people to see real economic progress coming out of the peace agreement with Israel. That is why there is no time to waste in setting up the economic framework for the new entity, and for the international community, the Israelis, the Jordanians, and other Arab countries to do their best to help the Palestinians ensure that it succeeds.

The Editors
Cambridge, Massachusetts

Introductory Note

Two thoughts have driven this project. In November 1991, as our conference on "The Economics of Middle East Peace" concluded, we realized that no one was preparing for an orderly transition in economic affairs between the status quo and the emergence of a new Palestinian entity. Officially, the parties had just begun to talk in Madrid; but they were not ready to engage seriously on economic affairs. We decided that the Institute should contribute to filling the void.

A second thought driving the project, one that came later, is that agreements on the issues on which we were working could become the bridging formula for an Israeli-Palestinian peace accord. Economics is a major sphere in which the two sides can test each other, prior to making final commitments.

Although the project was conceived at our Institute, it was the Israeli, Jordanian, and Palestinian economists who developed the structure and content for the project. The detailed agenda was theirs. They agreed on the subjects and the division of labor. The project belongs perhaps more to our colleagues from the region than it does to us at Harvard and the Massachusetts Institute of Technology (MIT). To our knowledge, this is the first document ever prepared by Israelis, Jordanians, and Palestinians.

Interactions among the three groups of economists during the project's eighteen months made for a fascinating process—and surprising personal metamorphoses. Several economists confessed that their initial participation was reluctant. One said that he actively had opposed the involvement of his colleagues—but said openly to the group, after ten hours of work, that his reluctance and opposition were misplaced. The economists moved from participation, to understanding each other's positions, to thinking from the perspectives of the others, and then even to making suggestions that might be helpful to those in the other parties.

At the very end, Palestinians were putting forth propositions that we expected from Israelis, and Israelis put forth propositions that we expected from Jordanians and Palestinians. The exhilarating discussions in our concluding three days of meetings (in February 1993) would have astonished observers.

We are extremely appreciative of the efforts on behalf of this project of the members of the Institute's board; other donors; political leaders on all three sides who supported us steadfastly; our colleagues at Harvard and MIT; and, most of all, our Israeli, Jordanian, and Palestinian colleagues who extended themselves in several ways on numerous occasions to ensure the successful conclusion of the project.

Leonard J. Hausman
Director

Anna D. Karasik
Associate Director
The Institute for Social and Economic Policy
in the Middle East

Acknowledgments

The recommendations of the report on the economics of transition in the West Bank and Gaza that follows can, we believe, help advance the peace process in the Middle East. The proposals have been generally agreed to by the Palestinian, Jordanian, Israeli and American economists who worked on this project. The recommendations are thoroughly practical—after all, no-one ever accused economists as a group of being excessively imaginative or sentimental—and many of them can be implemented in the near term, even as the peace negotiations proceed.

The report is presented at a number of levels. The busiest reader can get the major conclusions from the Executive Summary. We recommend that even this reader glance at Chapter 8, "The Way Ahead," for suggestions on how to begin immediately putting these recommendations into practice. Those with slightly more time can get a comprehensive overview of the report and its conclusions by reading Chapter 1, "Summary and Conclusions." Specialists will want to read the entire report.

The report is the product of a very large group of Israeli, Jordanian and Palestinian economists, working together with colleagues from Harvard and the Massachusetts Institute of Technology (MIT). Their names are listed below. We greatly appreciate having had the opportunity of working with them over the past 18 months. Not every meeting was completely amicable, but every meeting ended that way. We are grateful for the constructive spirit in which our teams worked, and for the efforts that team members made in putting together their reports, and in responding time and again to urgent requests for information and for comments. We have learned much from old and new friends, and we enjoyed the process of working with them—even as we occasionally marvelled to ourselves over the extraordinary fact that Palestinians, Jordanians, and Israelis were sitting down together to try to solve the problems posed by the economics of the peace process. We hope that they regard the final product as suitably reflecting their efforts and their intentions.

This was an immensely complicated project. The fundamental ideas were conceived by its Directors, Leonard Hausman and Anna Karasik, and the report would not exist but for their extraordinary devotion and abilities. They assembled the working groups of Israelis, Jordanians, and Palestinians, and that was no mean feat. And then they managed the even more difficult feat of making the trains run on time. The difficulty of that task can be judged by the fact that it was not possible to get even all the Harvard and MIT members together in one place at one time. Of course they managed the process of consensus-building towards the final report with unmatchable skill, humor, and patience. But most important, they played an essential role in creating the intellectual framework within which the report is written, and in working out many of its details.

Supporting their efforts at the Harvard Institute for Social and Economic Policy in the Middle East was a dedicated and able team: Bishara Bahbah, Susan Paulson, Walid Chamoun, Morris Arvoy, and David Lane. Alisa Rubin Peled and Michael Lee helped with editing and checking at the last stages.

We are grateful to all who contributed to this report, and commend the product of their efforts for your attention and action.

Stanley Fischer
Steering Committee Co-Chair, Project on the Economics of Transition

Thomas C. Schelling
Steering Committee Co-Chair, Project on the Economics of Transition
The Institute for Social and Economic Policy in the Middle East

Editorial Board

The Institute is very appreciative of the special efforts of the Editorial Board, who reviewed the Summary and Conclusions chapter. Editorial Board members are:

Tayseer Abdel Jaber

Haim Ben-Shahar

Maher El-Kurd

Chairs of Working Groups

Special thanks go to the professors of economics at Harvard University and the Massachusetts Institute of Technology (MIT) for chairing our several working groups. The professors are:

Stanley Fischer

Thomas C. Schelling

Richard B. Freeman

Dwight Perkins

Henry Rosovsky

Lester C. Thurow

Raymond Vernon

Participating Economists

Steering Committee

Co-Chairs
Stanley Fischer, *Massachusetts Institute of Technology (MIT), U.S.A.*
Thomas C. Schelling, *Harvard University, U.S.A.*

Members
Tayseer Abdel Jaber, *Former Executive Secretary, Economic & Social Commission of Western Asia, Jordan*

Mohamad Amerah, *Royal Scientific Society, Jordan*

Jawad Anani, *Jawad Anani Center for Economic Studies, Jordan*

Hisham Awartani, *An-Najah National University, West Bank*

Haim Ben-Shahar, *Tel-Aviv University, Israel*

Maher El-Kurd, *Palestine Liberation Organization, Tunisia*

Khaled El-Shuraydeh, *Higher Council for Science and Technology, Jordan*

Ghassan Khatib, *Jerusalem Media and Communications Center, West Bank*

Ephraim Kleiman, *Hebrew University, Israel**

Ruth Klinov, *Hebrew University, Israel*

*Prof. Kleiman joined the Steering Committee for the final meeting and preparation of the final report.

Mahmoud Okasha, *Al-Azhar University, Gaza*
Pinhas Zusman, *Hebrew University, Israel*

Alternates
Emanuel Sharon, *Bank Hapoalim, Israel*
Mohammed Shtayeh, *Birzeit University, West Bank*
Leonard J. Hausman, *Harvard University, U.S.A.*
Anna D. Karasik, *Harvard University, U.S.A.*

Regional Trade in Agriculture, Industry, and Services

Chair
Raymond Vernon, *Harvard University, U.S.A.*

Members
Omar M. Abdel-Raziq, *An-Najah National University, West Bank*
Abdel Rahman Al-Fataftah, *The Higher Council for Science and Technology, Jordan*
Hisham Awartani, *An-Najah National University, West Bank*
Ahmad Qassem El-Ahmad, *Royal Scientific Society, Jordan*
Mahmoud K. Okasha, *Al-Azhar University, Gaza*
Michael Michaely, *The World Bank, Israel*
Ezra Sadan, *Agriculture Research Institute, Volcani Center, Israel*

Labor Policies

Chair
Richard B. Freeman, *Harvard University, U.S.A.*

Members
Abdelfattah Abu-Shokor, *An-Najah National University, West Bank*
Ahmad Qassem El-Ahmad, *Royal Scientific Society, Jordan*
Ruth Klinov, *Hebrew University, Israel*

Economic Authority

Chair
Henry Rosovsky, *Harvard University, U.S.A.*

Members
Jawad Anani, *Jawad Anani Center for Economic Studies, Jordan*
Hisham Awartani, *An-Najah National University, West Bank*
Maher El-Kurd, *Palestine Liberation Organization, Tunisia*
John D. Montgomery, *Harvard University, U.S.A.*
Don Patinkin, *Hebrew University, Israel*
Emanuel Sharon, *Bank Hapoalim, Israel*
Mohammed Shtayeh, *Birzeit University, West Bank*

Fiscal Policy

Chair
Thomas C. Schelling, *Harvard University/University of Maryland,
U.S.A.*

Members
Atef Alawnah, *Al-Quds Open University, West Bank*
Daniel Gottlieb, *Bank of Israel, Israel*
Amin Haddad, *An-Najah National University, West Bank*
Khalil Hammad, *Yarmouk University, Jordan*
Ephraim Kleiman, *Hebrew University, Israel*
Efraim Sadka, *Tel-Aviv University, Israel*

Monetary and Financial Arrangements

Chair
Lester C. Thurow, *Massachusetts Institute of Technology (MIT),
U.S.A.*

Members
Ibrahim Affaneh, *Indiana University of Pennsylvania, U.S.A.*
Daniel Gottlieb, *Bank of Israel, Israel*
Khalil Hammad, *Yarmouk University, Jordan*
Hisham Jabr, *An-Najah National University, West Bank*
Leonardo Leiderman, *Tel-Aviv University, Israel*
Zvi Sussman, *Israel International Institute, Israel*

Management of Foreign Aid

Chair
Dwight Perkins, *Harvard University, U.S.A.*

Members
Avishay Braverman, *Ben-Gurion University of the Negev, Israel*
Hind Salman, *Bethlehem University, West Bank*
Munther A. Share', *Yarmouk University, Jordan*

Contributors

The Institute is grateful to those whose contributions principally underwrote this project: Mohammed Abudawood, Malcolm Brachman, the Charles R. Bronfman Foundation, Zein Mayassi, and the Rockefeller Foundation.

Other major donors were: The United States Institute of Peace, The European Commission, Leo Fields, the Joseph Meyerhoff Fund Inc., Leo Kahn, Henry Taub, and Joy Ungerleider.

For their significant contributions, we thank: Nicolas Chammas, Blaine L. Curtis, Hasan Ali Darwish, Max Factor III, Alan J. Gold, Joyce I. Greenberg, The Hauser Fund, Lewis Heafitz, Edmund Hoffman, Paul Homsy, Edwin Jaffe, Raymond Johnson, The Henry J. Kaiser Family Foundation, Nemir A. Kirdar, Melvyn Klein, Jonathan Kolber, Howard Kravets, Stephen Lebovitz, Leo Nevas, Morris Offit, Lyndon L. Olson, Jr., Irving Rabb, Bernard Rapoport, The Richard Ravitch Foundation, The Sheldon H. Solow Foundation, Jack Weingarten, and Norris Wolff.

XXVII

Executive Summary

Peace in the Middle East will be secured only when it takes root in the everyday lives of the people in the region. In addition to securing the appropriate political agreements, securing peace, therefore, requires establishing an hospitable environment for economic development.

Working with a team of economists from Harvard and the Massachusetts Institute of Technology (MIT), Palestinian, Israeli, and Jordanian economists present here a policy plan for trade and development among these three parties—a plan for the start of a new economic era in the Middle East.

The essential understandings in this report are: 1) that the formal peace treaties will grant the Palestinians economic sovereignty over an economy dominated by the private sector and one in which markets are the principal guide to the allocation of resources; 2) that the three economies will move towards free trade—with free trade between Israel and the Occupied Territories being largely attainable within a few months after the initial accords; and 3) that this is a fundamental transformation in existing economic relations, one that will be undergirded by regional projects integrating and benefiting the three economies.

The economics of peace should be comprehensive. The free trade arrangements could and should be widened to include as soon as possible Egypt, Lebanon, and Syria. In time, they could be extended further into an all-embracing Middle East Economic Community.

Regional Trade in Agriculture, Industry, and Services

We recommend that there be steady movement towards free trade and the free flow of capital among the three economies, with the goal of eventually achieving among them a free trade area in goods, services, capital, and technology. Free trade between Israel and the Occupied Territories can be reached very soon; between the Occupied Territories and Jordan more gradually; and between Israel and Jordan over a longer period. Special attention will have to be given to the early lifting of Israeli restrictions on Palestinian agricultural exports.

We recommend that working parties of experts should be appointed to develop regional projects in the following areas: tourist services; airport facilities; road and bridge facilities (including the need for road transportation within the Occupied Territories); and electric power.

While the World Bank has an important role to play, particularly in the next few years, we also recommend that a new regional bank be set up. This bank, the Middle Eastern Bank for Cooperation and Development (MEBCD), would have as its initial goal the development of regional projects involving the Palestinian, Jordanian, and Israeli economies. It could also be a vehicle for the financing of projects within the Occupied Territories. We believe strongly in functional cooperation and regard the MEBCD as an effective means of creating such cooperation.

Labor Policies

The short run priority is to promote job creation in the private sector in the Occupied Territories. We emphasize the importance for the labor market of all growth enhancing policies—increased investment, deregulation, and appropriate fiscal and monetary policies.

Even under the most optimistic scenarios, however, full employment requires that substantial numbers of Palestinians— at least 100,000—will need to continue to work in Israel. We therefore recommend the resumption of Palestinian access to the Israeli labor markets on the basis of agreed regulations and benefits.

We recommend consideration by the Palestinians of establishing a Palestinian "provident fund" as exists, for example, in Singapore. Under this system, which provides social insurance, individuals receive benefits that are related to their contributions. The provident fund could invest in private sector enterprises and projects. Such a scheme would need to be supplemented by social assistance funds.

To compensate Palestinians who work in Israel, and who pay social insurance taxes, but do not receive commensurate social insurance benefits, we offer two options: either to recompense workers directly, or to use these funds to support economic development in the Occupied Territories. For the future, the monies currently paid by employers could be paid into a Palestinian social insurance fund, whether that is a provident fund or some other mechanism that is established.

Economic Authority

We assume and recommend that within the framework of the negotiated agreement, the interim self-governing authority should be accorded effective legislative power regarding domestic economic matters. This should include not only power to issue new laws and regulations, but also authority to amend and abrogate laws inherited from previous authorities.

Our most important recommendation in the area of economic management is that the Palestinians should initially simply assume leadership of and utilize the existing institutions of Israel's Civil Administration for the West Bank and Gaza. Palestinians should replace Israeli military officers at the helm of these agencies, but existing bureaucracies and procedures should be left intact to provide an organized point of departure. From there on, the Palestinians obviously will develop their institutions of economic management in the directions they regard as most likely to promote economic development.

We recommend a new structure with four major economic management departments: Finance; Industry; Economic Development; and Human Resources. In addition to these four departments, we envisage a number of independent agencies, including the Central Bureau of Statistics and the Civil Service Administration. The Palestinian Interim Monetary and Financial Authority (PIMFA), responsible for the financial system, would likewise be run separately.

Fiscal Policy

The Palestinians appear now to be paying about 18% of GDP in taxes, half of which accrues to the Civil Administration. This is below, but not very much so, the average for an economy at this level of development. If arrangements are made for the Palestinians to recapture revenues (VAT and excise taxes) received by the Israeli government, the current tax apparatus could serve to generate revenues for the self-governing authority for a few years.

Spending in the public sector in the Occupied Territories, and especially infrastructure spending, is well below the normal levels, and should expand as the Palestinians take over their economy.

Partial, though not complete, harmonization of the VAT, and excise taxes and tariffs, will be needed, especially between the Occupied Territories and Israel. In each area, tax rates can differ somewhat, but not very much. Tariff harmonization would be easier if the Occupied Territories and Israel form a customs union. This would be facilitated by tariff rate reductions on the part of Israel.

Differences in corporate and personal income tax rates can be accommodated by agreements on taxation by country of residence of individuals and corporations.

Monetary and Financial Arrangements

We recommend that the dinar become legal tender in Gaza, and take it for granted that the extent of financial intermediation has to be expanded. During the transition period, it would be desirable for Israel to reduce capital controls further, at least to the point where they are no more restrictive than those of Jordan. All three economies would benefit from the free flow of capital.

The primary mission of the PIMFA will be to help improve the financial system in the Territories, and thereby contribute to their economic development. A separate agency is needed both because some of its tasks, such as bank supervision, require specialized knowledge, and also to ensure that a single institution is charged with this important responsibility. PIMFA's functions include:

• Chartering, supervision and regulation of new banks, as well as supervision and regulation of existing commercial banks;

• Chartering and supervision of non-bank financial intermediaries, such as insurance companies and pension funds;

• Collection and publication of data on the financial system; and advising the self-governing authority on macro-economic policy; and

• Shared responsibility for the creation and operation of needed public sector financial institutions and intermediaries (if any).

The Management of Foreign Aid

The role of foreign aid will be large and diverse, particularly in the early years while a public sector structure is being created and the private sector is being revitalized. Several different types of aid will be needed.

• Project Aid: Aid designated to support specific projects will be a major feature of assistance to the Occupied Territories for the indefinite future.

• Program Aid: This is general non-project financing, to fund the government budget, and for balance of payments support.

• Regional Projects: Foreign aid can play an essential role in the development of regional projects that involve several countries in the region.

The self-governing authority should set up an aid coordination agency, located in the Department of Finance, to coordinate, prepare requests for, and manage the implementation of, foreign aid.

During the transition period, and probably for several years thereafter, the self-governing authority is unlikely to have all the experience and skills required for the tasks it faces. Some of this experience gap can be filled by technical assistance.

Also needed for the Territories is an institution which will 1) make an appropriate assessment for the donors, and in conjunction with the Palestinian aid coordination agency, of the development needs and priorities within the Occupied Territories; 2) set up a framework to coordinate donor assistance, in conjunction with the Palestinian aid agency; 3) help manage general and project aid to the Occupied Territories; and 4) provide technical assistance to the self-governing authority. The leading international financial institution, the World Bank, is the natural and appropriate institution to take on these responsibilities initially. These responsibilities could gradually be taken over by the proposed regional development bank, the MEBCD.

There is also a role for a think-tank with experts from both inside and outside the Occupied Territories to provide counsel in the development of the economic plans for the area in general and the Territories in particular. This think-tank would complement, not compete with, the more regional perspective of analysts in the proposed regional bank.

1   Summary and Conclusions

Stanley Fischer and Thomas C. Schelling,
Steering Committee Co-Chairs

Peace in the Middle East will be secured only when it takes root in the everyday lives of the people of the region. That will happen if the peace brings open economic relations and economic development to the peoples and countries of the region—as it did in Western Europe after World War II.

The main conclusion of this report is that Israelis, Jordanians, and Palestinians can all benefit economically from an agreement in which:

• The Palestinians obtain control over the economy of the West Bank and Gaza;
• Substantially free trade develops among the three economies;
• Regional projects to develop the complementarities among the economies receive a high priority.

Each of the three economies ought to be market-friendly, relying on the private sector and market forces to play the leading role in allocating resources; and the private sectors of the three economies ought to be left free to develop commercial relations among them.

This report is the product of Palestinian, Jordanian, and Israeli economists, working together with economists from Harvard and the Massachusetts Institute of Technology (MIT).

The economists came to the project from different backgrounds, each committed to the well-being of his or her people, but each acting in this forum in an individual capacity. The participants shared two essential attributes: they all believed that there was more to be gained from cooperation than from continued confrontation; and they were all professionals, able to apply their professional skills to the solution of the concrete problems at hand.

The report deals with two interrelated sets of issues: first, future economic relations among the three economies; and second, the structure of the Palestinian economy as the interim period of self-government gets under way. There was some reticence among the Israeli and Jordanian economists about addressing questions that seemed to be internal Palestinian matters, such as the institutional structure for the management of the Palestinian economy. They were encouraged by their Palestinian colleagues to work on such issues—evidence of both the reality that the participants had much to offer each other, and the remarkably cooperative spirit in which the report was prepared.

This report is unique both because it is the joint product of Israelis, Jordanians, and Palestinians, and because it presents a non-official, forward-looking, professional appraisal of what can be done to put economics to work in the interests of peace in the Middle East. The appraisal is optimistic because there is reason for optimism.

We hope and believe that both the report and the spirit in which it was written will contribute to the economic development of the Palestinian, Jordanian, and Israeli economies, and thus to peace.

Process and Assumptions

This project was set up early in 1992 by the Institute for Social and Economic Policy in the Middle East of the John F. Kennedy School of Government.[1]

Its chief goal was to develop proposals for economic arrangements and policies that would best contribute to the economic development of the Palestinian, Jordanian, and Israeli economies during the transitional period of Palestinian autonomy envisaged as part of the peace process.

At the time the project was launched, peace talks between Israel and its neighbors were moving slowly. It was nonetheless possible for leading Israeli, Jordanian, and Palestinian economists to work together with American economists in an academic setting to analyze the possibilities for mutually beneficial economic relations among their economies.

The economists who prepared this report are listed in this report by name and institutional affiliation. They participated in their individual capacities; their views, as manifested here, are only their own. While relevant officials of the three parties involved in the peace talks have been kept informed about the project, we have not sought their approval for our recommendations.

There were several advantages to the way work on the project developed: its multilateral basis required all parties to understand the issues that confronted the others; its subject, the economics of transition, forced the group to focus on a relatively narrow topic; and the fact that the project was not official meant that the work was done away from the glare of publicity, enabling the participants to avoid the pressures placed on official representatives.

---

1. A detailed history of the project is presented in Appendix A.

As the project progressed, the peace process quickened, and work on the economics of transition and potential regional arrangements gathered momentum. Some members of our working groups were appointed as advisers to their delegations to the peace talks, but continued to participate in this unofficial project even as they took part in the official talks.

Central Assumptions

While the economists who fashioned this report concentrated on the technical economic aspects of the transitional arrangements, it was necessary to reach a common understanding of a political nature regarding both a starting and a finishing point.

The starting point is that the economists were to identify decisions to be made, problems to be solved, options to choose among, and policy recommendations where possible for the economic aspects of the transitional or interim period of Palestinian self-government. This starting point itself contains several assumptions. One is that there would be an agreement at some early date providing for a substantial change from the status quo in the political powers of the Palestinians and in their relationships with Israel and Jordan.

This change was reflected in the assumption that there would be created via a political agreement "a Palestinian entity with economic sovereignty." Hence, the economists were not working on new economic policies under the political status quo. Of course, an entity that engages in trade is likely to exercise that sovereignty to agree to mutual restraints, for example through agreements with its neighbors and the broader international community on trade and factor flows, and—as in the case of the European Community—other aspects of economic policy too.

The participants' basic and envisioned task did not include recommendations for the period following the transitional period. Nor did they make any assumptions about political arrangements after the transition, although of course some political outcomes were considered more likely than others. Rather than make a specific assumption about post-transition arrangements, the group assumed that economic policies for the interim period should be consistent with and facilitate any of the more likely political arrangements for the period after the transition. Having noted the central political assumption about the post-transition period, we acknowledge that many of our proposals, if implemented, would constrain political and economic options in the post-transition period.

The self-governing authority that is assumed to emerge from the peace talks is referred to initially in this report as the "Palestinian Interim Self-Governing Authority." After that initial reference, it is usually referred to as the interim self-governing authority or simply the self-governing authority. The land over which this authority exercises control is referred to interchangeably as the "West Bank and Gaza" and the "Occupied Territories."

The finishing point for the project is a conclusion, rather than an assumption, calling for market-friendly, private-sector based, development in the three economies, with extensive economic exchange among them.

We turn now to the substance of the report, starting with conclusions about relations among the three economies, and continuing with economic arrangements for the Palestinian entity. In each section of this summary chapter, we draw on the reports of the working groups in the different subject areas. The working group reports themselves are presented in Chapters 2 through 7 of the report.

Table 1.1
Selected Economic Characteristics of Israel, Jordan, and the West Bank and Gaza[a]

	Israel	Jordan[b]	Occupied Territories		
			W. Bank	Gaza	Combined
GDP (mil $)	59127	4083	1668	560	2228
GNP (mil $)	58989	3764	2134	864	2998
GDP per capita ($)	11962	1050	1700	850	1350
GNP per capita ($)	11878	968	2175	1310	1800
GDP by sector (%):					
Agriculture	2.4	8.3			20.6
Industry	21.8	26.5[c]			7.3
Construction	10.2				
Services	65.6	65.2			72.1[c]
Exports/GNP	30.6	29.8	10.5	13.3	11.3
Imports/GNP	46.2	66.2	29.3	34.8	30.9
Population (mil)	5.06	4.14	1.01[d]	0.68	1.69[d]

a. Figures for Israel and Jordan are for 1991. Total and per capita GNP and GDP figures for the Occupied Territories are averages of 1990 and 1991 figures.
b. Jordan's income for 1991 was low as a result of the Gulf War. In 1990, GDP per capita was $1340.
c. Includes construction.
d. Does not include East Jerusalem.

Sources: Data on Israel and West Bank and Gaza are from Central Bureau of Statistics, *Statistical Abstract of Israel*, 1992; Jordanian data are from Central Bank of Jordan, *Monthly Statistical Bulletin* (Vol. 28, No. 12, December 1992).

The Three Economies[2]

The differences in the starting circumstances of the three economies are striking. Basic data are presented in Table 1.1.

In 1991, Israeli GNP of $59 billion was about fifteen times that of Jordan,[3] and Jordan's was larger than that of the West Bank and Gaza. Israel's per capita GNP in 1991 was roughly $11,900 while that of Jordan was $1,000 (compared with $1,340 in 1990); per capita GNP in 1991 was $2,300 in the West Bank,

2. This section draws mainly on Chapter 2, the report of the group on Agriculture, Industry, Services and Trade.
3. Jordanian GNP was at a low point in 1991, as a result of the Gulf War and its aftermath.

and $1310 in Gaza, with the average income of the West Bank and Gaza being $1800. In 1991 almost a third of the GNP of the West Bank and Gaza derived from employment of residents of the territories in Israel. Reflecting this fact, GDP per capita in the West Bank was $1750 in 1990, and in Gaza it was only $850.

At present, Jordan does not trade with Israel. Jordan's modest trade with the Occupied Territories leaves the latter with a small merchandise trade surplus vis-à-vis Jordan. Israel trades extensively with the West Bank and Gaza; it has a large trade surplus in goods with the Territories, which is to a considerable extent offset by Israeli purchases of Palestinian labor services.[4] While Israel's overall economic dependence on the Occupied Territories is small, both by overall degree of dependence on Palestinian labor and in relation to total output, both Israeli agriculture and construction are heavily dependent on Palestinian labor. These patterns have, of course, been the result of the Israeli occupation of the Territories.

The domestic markets of each of the three economies are too small for an inward-oriented development strategy to succeed. With import substitution ruled out as a serious possibility for a take-off strategy, development policy will have to rely on an export-oriented strategy. This has to a great extent been recognized in Israel, where the export sector has played a leading role in growth, and which has negotiated free trade arrangements with both the United States and Europe.

It is often pointed out that the economies of the northern Middle East lack the oil and other natural resources on the basis of which incomes in the Gulf countries have grown in the past two decades. But one lesson of post-World War II development, especially in East Asia, is that natural resources are not essential for growth. Rather export-oriented strategies, combined with

---

4. As a result of events in December 1992, Israel reduced sharply the number of Palestinians employed in Israel. Whether this policy will continue is unclear.

education to create a skilled labor force, have succeeded all over the world.

Given the shared borders of the three economies, there would normally be extensive trade and investment among them. Obviously politics have distorted these patterns: trade between Jordan and Israel has been prohibited; there is extensive trade between Israel and the Territories; trade between the West Bank and Gaza and Arab countries, including Jordan, has been restrained.

Obviously, it is the prerogative of the interim self-governing authority to make the choice between free trade (and the rise in income it will bring) and economic isolation (and the lesser prosperity is will bring). We recommend that there be steady movement on the basis of voluntary arrangements agreed to by the parties, towards free trade and the free flow of capital among the three parties, with the goal of eventually achieving among them a free trade area in goods, services, capital, and technology. But we must emphasize the differences in current trading relations among the economies. Israel and the West Bank and Gaza are relatively close to free trade; its attainment would take Israeli removal of the many serious restrictions on Palestinian exports from the West Bank and Gaza. It will take a longer time, and more changes, for free trade to take place between Jordan and the West Bank and Gaza; and free trade between Israel and Jordan would require extensive changes in their trading regimes. Since the West Bank and Gaza do not now have their own trade restraints, progress towards free trade would require actions by Israel and Jordan, and mainly restraint from the West Bank and Gaza.[5]

Presumably, any agreements among Israel, Jordan, and the West Bank and Gaza governing the conduct of the parties in

---

5. Of course, the exercise of restraint in trade policy requires tough decisions when the inevitable protectionist pressures begin to appear.

trade and investment will be asymmetrical in the early years, allowing greater tolerance for government-sponsored promotional measures on the part of the West Bank and Gaza than for their more developed partners in such agreements. Such tolerance would be particularly important as long as the West Bank and Gaza did not have the option of devaluing a national currency.

An obvious question is whether customs posts will be opened at the borders between Israel and the Occupied Territories. That would set up a potential dynamic that ends with extensive import restrictions in both directions. The absence of customs posts would provide the best assurance of the free flow of goods between the economies of Israel and the West Bank and Gaza. While this is a desirable outcome, we fear that political and economic adjustment pressures in the two economies make it unlikely. If, unfortunately, interim trade restrictions are permitted, it will be important to agree to limit their applicability, and to recognize firmly from the very first that the ultimate goal should be achieving the elimination of border restrictions on the flow of capital, goods, and technology in the industrial sector.

The creation of a free trade area among the three economies will require several different negotiations. As we have noted, in many ways a free-trade area already exists between Israel and the Occupied Territories: the negotiation of trade arrangements between the two economies that protect and extend the existing free movement of goods, while removing the coercion that exists in the current arrangements, should be possible as part of the peace process. On the Israeli side, these negotiations will have to make room for Palestinian exports of goods in which they have a comparative advantage, including agricultural goods and textiles. A period of transition may be required to ease the Israeli adjustments to these changes, but the changes

will have to be made if the potential gains from trade in the
region are to be realized.

Given the importance of labor flows to the Palestinian economy, and the importance of improved Palestinian economic performance to the success of the peace, we strongly recommend
the resumption of labor flows from the West Bank and Gaza to
Israel.[6] The Palestinians and Israelis may agree to regulate conditions of work for the Palestinian laborers and perhaps limit
the total flow, but any sharp cutback from the 100,000 level that
prevailed before the Intifada would unnecessarily increase economic hardship in the Territories.

It should be possible to reach agreement within a short time,
say no more than a year, on moving towards free trade across a
broad range of goods between Jordan and the Palestinian entity.
However, the achievement of broad-scale free trade between
Israel and Jordan would take longer, for Jordanian firms have
not until now been subject to Israeli competition. Generally, the
smaller economy in a free trade agreement will eventually benefit more from the lifting of trade restrictions, but any economic
restructuring imposes transitional costs that will have to be recognized and allowed for. With good will, Israel and Jordan can
gradually move to open their economies to each other.

The overlap within a Palestinian entity of Israel-Palestinian
and Jordan-Palestinian free trade agreements will inevitably
make it difficult to control goods flows between Israel and
Jordan—and among these countries and their respective trading
partners. While rules of origin can provide a basis for regulating
trade in these circumstances, such regulations are easily circum-
vented. It is quite likely that unofficial trade between Israel and
Jordan, and perhaps the rest of the Arab world, would gradually develop through the West Bank and Gaza, even in the
absence of explicit trade agreements. Because such trade would

---

6. Labor issues are discussed in Chapter 3.

spur market-opening trade negotiations between Israel and Jordan, we regard the possibility with equanimity.

The economic development of the Occupied Territories will benefit from increased trade with countries other than Jordan and Israel. Provision will have to be made for the Palestine entity to set up trade relations with countries in the Arab world and elsewhere. The European Community has already indicated that it will be willing to grant favored access to goods from the Territories, and that possibility should be vigorously pursued.

The trading relations of the West Bank and Gaza during the past quarter century have been politically constrained. Normally the Territories would be expected to trade relatively more with Middle Eastern countries other than Israel than they do now. It is quite likely in the event of peace that trade between the Territories and Arab countries will expand far more rapidly than trade between Israel and the Territories. Israel should view this change as a return to a more normal situation, rather than a challenge to the peace process.

Regional Cooperation

It is increasingly being recognized that the transborder flow of services represents a critical part of the international interaction required for the successful development of industry and trade. In the case of Israel, Jordan, and a Palestinian entity, the services that will prove of immediate interest in an era of self-government are tourist services, transportation (including especially airports and buses), electric power, and banking; eventually, some of the licensed professions, such as engineers, physicians, and accountants may be added to the list.

These activities are also of importance because some of them offer special opportunities for direct collaboration among the parties in the region. Tourist services provide a particularly strong opportunity because of the potential importance of that sector to a self-governed West Bank and Gaza. Although successful collaboration in tourism will depend fundamentally on enterprises in the private sector, governmental agreements to facilitate transportation and border crossings will also play a significant role. (There is also room in this area for collaboration with Egypt, and Syria and Lebanon as well.)

Each regulated service area in which constructive cooperation seems possible should be taken up in a committee of experts, with the object of producing realistic programs for cooperation among the parties. We recommend, therefore, that working parties of experts, operating under a strong mandate to reduce national barriers to transborder movements, should be appointed in the following areas: tourist services, airport and seaport facilities, bus facilities, road and bridge facilities, and electric power. We include under road and bridge facilities the need to improve road transportation between the West Bank and Gaza.

A Regional Development Bank

At the request of the multilateral peace meetings, the World Bank has already been working on the economies of the region, with an emphasis on the potential for regional cooperation. With its wealth of experience and resources, the World Bank obviously has an important role to play in coordinating aid and providing technical assistance to countries in the region.

Because membership in the World Bank is limited to states, the interim self-governing authority will not be able to become a member. However, with some ingenuity and goodwill, and given the support of relevant countries, it should be possible for the international financial institutions to provide advice and channel financing to the West Bank and Gaza. Trust funds donated by other countries in the region and elsewhere are the most promising avenue through which the World Bank and other international agencies could assist the development of the Palestinians.

While the World Bank has an important role to play, particularly in the next few years, we also recommend that a new regional bank be set up. This bank, the Middle Eastern Bank for Cooperation and Development (MEBCD)—its name a mixture of the IBRD (International Bank for Reconstruction and Development) and OECD (Organization for Economic Cooperation and Development)—would have as its initial goal the development of regional projects involving the Palestinian, Jordanian and Israeli economies, but could include as members from the outset other countries from the region. While we have not recommended favorably on the prospect of a Palestinian development bank—because such institutions have not been effective elsewhere—we believe that this is a matter on which the interim self-governing authority must pass judgement. It could also be a vehicle for the financing of projects within the West Bank and Gaza.

The case for the creation of the MEBCD is that it is crucial to the deepening of peace in the Middle East that the peoples of the area learn to work together. The Bank should be run by experienced and high quality professionals from all member countries. But because a major goal would be to encourage people from different parts of the region to learn to work together, there should be a preference for staffing the bank with residents of the region. This would help ensure that citizens of the region work together on concrete, technical issues, on projects yielding net benefits for all parties. We believe strongly in *functional cooperation*, and regard the MEBCD as an effective means of creating such cooperation.

The MEBCD would be financed through capital contributions by member countries. It would have a regular development banking function, borrowing in international capital markets and lending at market rates to projects likely to earn market rates of return. It could also have special funds lent on more concessional terms much like the International Development Association of the World Bank. By channeling funds through this regional bank, donors would have more confidence that the funds would be well used than would be the case with many bilateral projects.

If the MEBCD is set up, and includes Palestinians, Israelis and Jordanians among its leadership and staff, it will provide a powerful signal of a new spirit of cooperation and creativity in the region. If the Bank succeeds, we would expect it also to become the forum for discussions and negotiations on issues and policies that concern all three economies, in the way the OECD now serves as a forum for analysis and discussion of the issues confronting the major industrialized countries. In time, we would also expect the Bank to expand geographically, to take in Lebanon, Syria and Egypt, and then other nations in the Middle East wishing to participate.

The Structure of the Palestinian Economy[7]

The Palestinian economy is more agricultural and less industrial than those of its neighbors; it relies heavily on the export of labor services to Israel and other countries, notably in the Gulf. The economy is correspondingly vulnerable to disruptions such as those caused by the Gulf War and by Israeli restrictions on labor inflows from the Territories.

---

7. We draw in this section mainly on the Report on Agriculture, Industry, Services and Trade (Chapter 2).

Agriculture

Agriculture has been of critical importance to the Occupied Territories, with the West Bank heavily committed to the production of olives and Gaza to citrus fruit. The agricultural sector contributes about 25 percent to the GDP of the Territories, with substantial variations from one year to the next mainly due to variations in the value of the olive crop. Agriculture absorbs 23 percent of the Palestinian labor force, and accounts for 60 percent of the exports of goods.

Unlike in Israel and Jordan, the agriculture of the West Bank and Gaza has not been protected from the competition of neighbors. In earlier years, the Israeli agricultural extension services helped introduce technological developments in agriculture in the Territories. However, in recent years agriculture in the West Bank and Gaza has not received much direct governmental support either in technology or in marketing. Restrictions on water use, inferior support services, and restrictions imposed by the Israeli military and on exports to Israel have limited the possibilities of raising the productivity and increasing the market opportunities of producers in these areas.

Despite these difficulties, the proximity of the Israeli and Jordanian markets has been and will continue to be a real stimulus for Palestinian agriculture. Some products not produced in adequate quantities by Israeli producers have been admitted to Israel, while others have been moved clandestinely into Israeli markets in arrangements often developed jointly with Israeli distributors. Jordan, too, has allowed the importation of some goods in these categories, enough to generate a negative trade balance with the West Bank and Gaza. The agriculture of the West Bank and Gaza is to a considerable extent complementary to that of Israel.

The long term objective in agriculture among the cooperating countries should be that of free trade. However, an agreement to move towards free trade in agricultural products cannot mean instantaneous transition from a state of restricted trade to one of open borders. After a long history of protection in the agricultural sectors of both Israel and Jordan, interim arrangements involving a phasing out of trade restrictions and subsidies have to be negotiated and agreed upon jointly. Otherwise, it is likely that protection in agriculture will persist for a long time. Interim arrangements may entail more rapid movement towards unrestricted trade between Israel and the Occupied Territories than between the West Bank and Gaza and Jordan and between Israel and Jordan. A Palestinian entity will also want to develop direct agricultural links with other economies.

The development of West Bank and Gaza agriculture will require cooperation with the neighboring economies in a wide range of areas, most critically water rights. Progress in that direction will demand serious attention to this issue within the peace talks. In addition the water authorities in each of the areas should begin pricing that commodity in a closer relationship to its real market value. Once the issue of water distribution is effectively addressed, the parties will be in a far better position to improve their use of the existing water resources of the region and to mobilize international efforts for the purpose of increasing total supply.[8]

With a fair agreement on water use in hand, the self-governing authority will be able to proceed to develop irrigation schemes for agriculture. For this purpose it should be able to draw on both Israeli and Jordanian expertise, and that of the international institutions. The effective use of irrigation will

---

8. Work on water issues is proceeding in a related project at the Institute for Social and Economic Policy in the Middle East; its report will be available later.

require the provision of power to the agricultural sector. In addition, agricultural development in the West Bank and Gaza will require improved transportation, storage, and other infrastructure and credit facilities.

The creation of transportation infrastructure within the West Bank and Gaza will be the responsibility of the self-governing authority, while facilities for transporting exports will have to be designed in collaboration with the neighboring economies.

Agricultural research and extension has played a key role in increasing productivity, and research should be directed to the special needs of Palestinian agriculture. There would be many advantages to the creation of an agricultural research center in the West Bank and Gaza. It would be natural and desirable for such an institution to work in close collaboration with agricultural research facilities in Israel and Jordan, and also to draw on international expertise.

To help achieve these ends, we recommend that as an integral part of the peace process, a high level committee composed of representatives of the parties should jointly map out the steps for the promotion of free agricultural trade among the three entities. It should also make recommendations and reach decisions in those areas identified above, including water, where joint action among the entities is needed.

Industry

Industrial establishments account for about 9 percent of the labor force working in the West Bank and 14 percent of the labor force working in Gaza. Most of the manufacturing establishments of the Occupied Territories are small, approximating cottage industries. The typical enterprise is family-owned and family-managed, with its capital resources coming from inside

the family; indeed, less than 10 percent of total industrial investment in the West Bank and Gaza comes from commercial banks
or other visible financial intermediaries.

Industrial production in the West Bank and Gaza is significantly dependent on the Israeli economy: four out of every ten
industrial workers are employed in the production of textiles,
clothing and leather products, industries composed largely of
subcontractors to Israeli enterprises. Reliance of industrial activity in small economies on subcontracting and exports is common, especially in early stages of industrial development, and
would be likely to continue in the West Bank and Gaza so long
as the economies of the region remain open to each other.

The development of the industrial sector of the West Bank
and Gaza has been blocked by various factors: a licensing policy
that discouraged the establishment of large industrial enterprises (abandoned as of the beginning of 1991, according to Israel);
military restraints on the movement of materials into and out of
the territories; limited local banking for the financing of local
industry; restraints on the development of free trade zones,
other industrial zones, and related infrastructure; and restraints
on the development of supporting public institutions.

These policies have exacerbated the inherent problems of the
area, such as the limited size of the local market and the lack of
industrial training and experience of its people. The policies of
Jordan in maintaining tight controls over West Bank exports,
and uncertainties over access for Palestinian products to the
Israeli market, have added to the difficulties.

Industrial development policy for the West Bank and Gaza
will have to rely on an export-oriented strategy. Such a strategy
would have two essential components: first, Palestinian entrepreneurs and the self-governing authority would seek to
improve the access of their industry and agriculture to export
markets—in the Middle East, in Europe, and North America,

and to encourage exports; and second, they would seek to attract foreign capital—from Palestinians abroad and other sources—and technology to invest in the West Bank and Gaza.

If the West Bank and Gaza are granted improved access to other markets including Israel and Jordan, it would be possible to begin to attract foreign investment. Beyond the emotional attachment that might initially attract capital from Palestinians abroad, the attractions for such potential investors would be the availability of a well-educated labor force and the accessibility of other markets, especially in the Middle East and Europe, from production and trading bases in the West Bank and Gaza. The self-governing authority would also have to provide competitive (with other economies) benefits to foreign investors, with the aim of capturing the externalities they may bring. Such results require that indigenous entrepreneurship and training should be supported and encouraged at the same time.

While we strongly support a policy that encourages industry, exports and foreign investment in general, we equally strongly advise against a policy that would seek to support particular industries, by picking winners. Our development experience has left us more impressed by the difficulty of predicting which industries will emerge than by past successes in doing so.

Labor Markets[9]

The close proximity of the West Bank and Gaza to the important Israeli labor markets, coupled with the less developed state of the domestic Palestinian economy, has resulted in the extensive dependence of Palestinian workers on employment in Israel. Until recent months, one-third of the Palestinian labor force held jobs in Israel. Despite their close proximity, and for obvious political reasons, Israelis and Jordanians do not work

---

9. We draw here on the material in Chapter 3.

in each other's labor markets; and Palestinians residing in the Occupied Territories are not permitted to hold jobs in Jordan.

Underutilization of labor plagues the Israeli, Jordanian, and Palestinian economies. In Israel, unemployment has risen from 4.8 percent in 1980 to 10.8 percent in 1991. In good part, this is attributable to Soviet immigration into Israel. In the West Bank, the sum of unemployment, involuntary part-time employment, and absenteeism have risen from 12.8 percent in 1980 to 25.3 percent in 1991; while the corresponding figures for Gaza are 9.0 and 19.3 percent. A recession and the Intifada are the major explanatory factors here. Jordan reports a rise in unemployment from 4.3 percent in 1982 to 19 percent in 1991, a result of a tidal wave of returning Jordanians and Palestinians compelled to leave the Gulf after the war there.

Responding to the social tensions resulting from rising labor underutilization, both Israelis and Palestinians prefer a shift in Palestinian employment from Israel to the Palestinian entity. If even larger scale unemployment and poverty in the West Bank and Gaza than currently obtain are to be avoided, the employment of large numbers of Palestinians in Israel is essential. Israeli demand for Palestinian workers is already declining because of frictions, competition in jobs for Palestinians on the part of Soviet immigrants, and a decline in the Israeli construction industry. The domestic demand for Palestinian workers may rise as their economy is freed of Israeli constraints and trade opens up.

The realities of the domestic Palestinian labor market, however, are these. The annual rate of growth in Palestinian job-seekers is 9,000; while the annual growth of new jobs is 4,000. Thus, there is a job deficit annually of 5,000, and this deficit accumulates in the absence of other changes. To add to the need for domestic job creation, an agreement in the peace talks could allow for the return of some refugees. At this point, the number of returning refugees is a matter of speculation. If workers returning from the Israeli labor market are added to returning refugees, the pressure of unemployment could grow to dangerous levels.

This report calls centrally and emphatically for steady movement towards free trade in goods and services among Israel, Jordan, and the West Bank and Gaza. Our recommendations with regard to labor flows are more complicated. We support the continuation of labor flows from the West Bank and Gaza into Israel, and recommend strongly against any attempts to cut back on such flows too quickly; doing so will increase unemployment and poverty in the West Bank and Gaza, and is likely therefore to enhance political radicalization. Private sector job opportunities in the West Bank and Gaza for Palestinian workers need to be expanded, but it is not possible to do so very rapidly. That will take a build-up of investment.

We recommend against a rapid opening of the weak Jordanian labor market to Palestinians. This will drive down wages and increase tensions there.

A second important area for policy development on labor relates to social insurance. While Palestinians hired through Israeli employment offices pay social insurance taxes, they do not receive commensurate benefits. The Palestinians are eligible for National Insurance benefits in Israel in the event of work-related accidents and severance pay in the event of their firm's bankruptcy. These workers are not entitled to old-age pensions, unemployment insurance, and child allowances.

Our estimate is that over the past 25 years, the maximum, cumulative differences between the social insurance contributions paid by Palestinians and the benefits they received was $250 million (ignoring interest). The questions are what to do both about compensation for this difference, and policy for the future. The Israeli government states that a substantial part of this $250 million was remitted annually to the budget of the

Civil Administration, and thus should be deducted from the sum; however, the government has not produced data on this.[10]

To the extent that some of the past balances are recognized as insurance over-payments by Palestinians working in Israel, the amounts due to them could either be transferred in their name to a Palestinian Provident Fund if, as recommended below, it is established; or paid to them in cash; or granted to them as retroactive insurance rights in Israel; or a combination of the three. The same options are open for the future: namely, to establish a Palestinian Provident Fund, to which monies currently paid by employers would be given in the name of each worker; to credit Palestinian workers with their contributions in the Israeli social insurance system; or to reduce their contributions.

If, on the other hand, past balances are treated as taxes, they could be destined for a general purpose, e.g. to finance development in the West Bank and Gaza or provide the initial funding for a Palestinian Provident Fund.

We recommend serious consideration by the Palestinian self-governing authority and its Department of Finance of establishing a Palestinian "Provident Fund," as exists in Singapore. Under the Provident Fund system, individuals receive benefits in accord with their contributions: benefits received are a function of contributions and interest on invested contributions. There are no interpersonal transfers.

Two key questions are the types of risks covered by the Provident Fund and the level of contributions. Although initially per capita income will be low in the emerging Palestinian entity, we suggest that the fund cover the risks of low income in old age, work related accident insurance, and health insurance. Consistent with what has been argued in the paper presented in

---

10. The Civil Administration's revenues and expenditures for 1993 will be made available, following an Israeli Supreme Court ruling in the week of May 24, 1993.

this report on fiscal affairs, benefits in the area ought to be limited so that contributions can be kept at a tolerable level at the outset. As Palestinian per capita income grows, benefits and contributions should be increased. In due course, contributors to the Provident Fund should be required to use a fraction of their personal endowment in the Fund to purchase annual health insurance premia, and permitted or required to use another fraction for the purchase of housing. This assumes growth in per capita incomes and, correspondingly, contribution rates to the Fund.

A particular advantage of the Provident Fund is that it encourages personal savings. If rates of return on domestic investment are high, these savings can be channeled into private sector activities that will create domestic jobs for Palestinian workers. We underscore the importance of creating private sector jobs within the West Bank and Gaza for Palestinian workers.

Economic Authority[11]

We assume and recommend that within the framework of the negotiated agreement, the interim self-governing authority should be accorded effective legislative power regarding domestic economic matters. This should include not only the power to issue new laws and regulations, but also authority to amend and abrogate laws inherited from previous authorities (Ottoman, British, Jordanian, and Israeli).

At the start of the period of self-government, the Palestinians will have to put in place an institutional structure through which to manage both the economy of the West Bank and Gaza, and the coordination of policies between the Palestinians and their economic partners, Israel and Jordan.

---

11. This section summarizes the contents of Chapter 4.

Our most important recommendation in this area is that the Palestinians should initially simply assume leadership of and utilize the existing institutions of the Israel Civil Administration for the West Bank and Gaza. Palestinians should replace Israeli military officers at the helm of these agencies, but the existing bureaucracies and procedures should be left intact to provide an organized point of departure. From there on, the Palestinians obviously will develop their institutions of economic management in the directions they regard as most likely to promote economic development.

While we do not specify details of the transition between the initial structure and that at the end of the period of interim self-government, we believe the changeover should be gradual, and based on careful studies of the needs of the new self-governing authority.

We recommend a new structure with four major economic management departments: a Department of Finance; Department of Industry, Trade and Tourism; Department of Economic Development; and Department of Human Resources.

The *Department of Finance* would be the central economic department. Its main responsibility would be the presentation and management of the annual budget. It would thus need to set and coordinate the priorities for government spending, and to provide the revenue to finance government outlays. The department would develop an internal revenue service, and the Palestinian social protection system. The Finance Department would also begin to consider macro-economic fiscal policy. For this purpose it might want to set up a bureau of policy and planning.

In light of the likely importance of foreign aid to the Palestinian economy in its early years, we recommend that the management of foreign aid be assigned to a special agency in the Department of Finance. The Foreign Aid Agency would manage all foreign aid operations, negotiating with donors and coordinating with the budget planning bureau.

The *Department of Industry, Trade and Tourism* would be responsible for the promotion and regulation of international trade, and in that context would administer trade regulations. These should include the promotion of exports from the West Bank and Gaza, an area where international technical expertise can be mobilized. The department might also eventually collect customs fees and duties. Such departments often become strong forces for protection, and it would be important in establishing regulations to try to ensure that they do not unnecessarily impede international trade.

The department would supervise joint ventures and other economic activities with foreign countries. It would establish and regulate product standards. It might encourage the development of industrial and free trade zones, and coordinate its work with chambers of commerce. Finally, it would control and regulate the use of land and the environment.

The *Department of Economic Development* would direct economic development policy and the provision of infrastructure for a market-oriented, private-enterprise dominated Palestinian economy. It would be necessary for this department to coordinate closely with the Department of Finance and the Department of Industry, Trade and Tourism (DITT), so that development and infrastructure planning is consistent with the promotion of the private sector that will be the main focus of the DITT. Planning would also have to be consistent with the availability of financing, which is the responsibility of the Department of Finance.

This department would include, in addition to a development planning bureau, several sectoral bureaus, for instance transportation, communications, energy and agriculture.

An alternative arrangement is possible in which these three departments are consolidated into two, with the development planning function included in the finance department, and the sectoral bureaus in the DITT.

The *Department of Human Resources* would manage a wide variety of essential activities pertaining to the Palestinian labor force inside and outside the self-governed area; and the management of returning refugees, as agreed to in the politically-negotiated agreement. Its bureaus would include education, training, absorption and registration, and labor standards.

In addition to these four departments, we envisage a number of independent agencies, including the Central Bureau of Statistics; the Civil Service Administration (including a public administration institution); and a scientific research and technology council. The *Palestinian Interim Monetary and Financial Authority* (PIMFA), responsible for the financial system, would likewise be run separately; it is described below.

Finally, since the economies of Israel, Jordan, and the Palestinian entity are likely to be so intertwined with one another, there will be a need for on-going coordination. The need for such coordination is self-evident. For instance, value added taxes that are not harmonized would have adverse consequences for legitimate cross-border trade; and so would differences in trade regulations with respect to third parties. External aspects of coordination could be handled initially by a "high liaison coordinating council" consisting of representatives of Jordan, the Palestinian entity, and Israel.

Fiscal Policy[12]

Palestinians currently pay about 18 percent of GDP in taxes, half of this accruing to the Civil Administration, the remainder being paid to the Government of Israel in the form of value added tax and import duties. This share of taxes is below the

---

12. This section summarizes the material of Chapter 5.

average for countries at the income levels of the West Bank and Gaza, but not very much so. Nonetheless, we conclude that the self-governing authority could probably use the existing tax system (which includes income and value added taxes) in its early years, without necessarily undertaking a major tax reform.

Expenditures by the Civil Administration and municipalities amount to only 15 percent of GDP, well below comparable levels elsewhere. Development and capital spending by government in the Occupied Territories is particularly low.

The general conclusion of this report, that it is desirable to move towards free trade among the neighboring economies, imposes constraints on tax and tariff policies among the economies. The two principal kinds of tax issues that need to be considered can be briefly characterized as *tax coordination* and *revenue recovery*.

Tax coordination is needed because significant tax differences on similar goods cannot exist in an economic region as small as Israel and the Palestinian entity without diverting customers in large numbers from the higher to the lower tax region. Not only is such diversion wasteful of consumer time, but it can lead to "tax competition" between the two tax regions, as has been observed frequently in the United States, and as is recognized in the moves to coordinate value added taxation in Europe. Thus, some coordination of tax rates will be required between Israel, the West Bank and Gaza, and Jordan, as trade with the latter develops.

The problem of revenue recovery is illustrated by the present payment of over $100 million in VAT by Palestinians to the Israeli tax authorities, on their net imports from Israel. As a result, Palestinian consumers are paying more VAT to Israeli fiscal authorities than vice versa. If the object of the VAT is to tax consumption, then Israel is taxing Palestinian consumption more than the West Bank and Gaza is taxing Israeli consumption.

Similarly, when Palestinians purchase goods imported through Israel from the rest of the world, the import duties collected by the Israeli authorities are ultimately paid for by the Palestinian final purchaser. Both the VAT and customs duties generate net revenues for Israel which are paid by Palestinians; therefore, a negotiated formula for recovering these revenues is clearly called for.

Coordination of customs duties will also be required. Even a small differential between the tariffs of Israel and the self-governing authority could reroute imports through the lower tariff area, thus avoiding the customs regime of the other. This problem is avoided in a customs union, the members of which specify a common external tariff, and agree on a basis for sharing the tariff revenues. The problem is far more difficult in a free trade area, whose members permit free trade with each other while permitting differences in tariffs against non-members.

It would certainly be easier for Israel and the Palestinians to maintain free trade if they continued, as now, with a common external tariff. Israel would make a customs union more attractive for the Palestinians, and for Jordan as well, if it proposed an equitable basis for sharing customs revenues. Maintenance of a customs union would also be much more likely if Israel sharply speeded up its proposed tariff reforms against non-EC, non-US goods. Agreement between the Palestinians and Israel on very low or zero tariffs against goods from Jordan and the rest of the Arab world would further enhance the likelihood of maintenance of a customs union. In due course, there could be an Israeli-Jordanian-Palestinian customs union.

There is less need for coordination of income tax rates. While there is always the risk of the Palestinian entity providing a tax shelter for Israeli and Jordanian firms and vice versa, agreements can be negotiated under which the income of Jordanian-owned (Israeli-owned) corporations registered in the Territories is deemed to be produced in Jordan (Israel) and is subject to tax under the Jordanian (Israeli) rates; alternatively, Jordan (Israel) can tax the income of Jordanian (Israeli) firms operating in the Palestinian entity and allow a foreign tax credit against taxes paid in the Territories. Similarly, with personal income taxes, an agreement will be required to prevent double taxation and to provide mutual disclosure of cross-residencies.[13]

From the point of view of taxation, what kind of social security system should be contemplated during the transition and what should be its ultimate goal? Because income per capita in the Palestinian entity will, for many years, perhaps even decades, be substantially lower than that of neighboring Israel, the system will have to be modest.

In searching for a social security system, the Palestinians should look both close and far. Close by is the Jordanian example. That system displays several characteristics worth noticing. One is that, in the private sector, the social protection system began with modest coverage and progressively extended its coverage, as was the case in many countries including the United States. A second characteristic is that certain kinds of employment and employees are more readily extended coverage than others; thus, for example, regular workers in large plants are more easily integrated into the system than domestic servants, the self-employed, sailors, fishermen, and farmers. Furthermore, the Jordanian system is imbedded in a Muslim tradition that provides charitable contributions outside the official social security system.[14] Further afield, we have already rec-

---

13. The special problem that arises with respect to social security taxes levied on Palestinians working in Israel has already been discussed.

14. Particulars on the nature of the social protection system were offered above in Section IV.

ommended the creation of a provident fund, along lines similar to that of Singapore, but with modifications to reflect the social traditions and the development level of the Palestinian economy.

A survey of infrastructure needs to identify projects, and their levels of urgency and priority will be important for the interim government; it can also help to measure the magnitude of the fiscal problem. While we do not have a comprehensive framework within which to estimate infrastructure needs, extrapolation of some information available to us suggests, as an exceedingly rough order of magnitude, infrastructure investment needs of $3 billion over ten years, or an average of $300 million in 1993 dollars per year. That kind of figure needs to be fitted into the fiscal framework and the prospects for foreign aid over the coming decade. Infrastructure is of course an area likely to be attractive to providers of foreign aid.

Monetary and Financial Arrangements[15]

The single most important fact about the financial system in the West Bank and Gaza is that the amount of financial intermediation between lenders and borrowers is very small, even though residents hold large amounts of financial assets. The rate of saving in the Territories fluctuates but is on average high; accumulated savings in the form of financial assets and in the form of housing is high,[16] but very little formal lending takes place. The key ingredient for an active financial system, savings, is already present. There is thus no major impediment to the development of an active and efficient financial system in the West Bank and

---

15. We draw here on Chapter 6, "Financial and Monetary Arrangements in the Palestinian Transition."

16. Financial assets in the form of M2 exceed 40 percent of GNP, a level that is high by international standards.

Gaza if the right climate for investment and for the development of the financial system is created.

Current financial and monetary arrangements reflect the results of Israeli policy since 1967. Before the 1967 war, the Jordanian dinar was the legal tender in the West Bank, and the Egyptian pound was the legal tender in Gaza. Now both the Israeli shekel and the dinar are legal tender on the West Bank, while only the shekel is legal tender in Gaza. The dinar is also widely used in Gaza.

In May 1967 there were 31 bank branches in the West Bank and East Jerusalem. These banks were closed after the 1967 War, and Israeli banks were opened. In September 1986, the Cairo-Amman Bank was reopened on the West Bank, after a tacit agreement between the central banks of Jordan and Israel. It has branches in Nablus, Ramallah (two), Jenin, Tulkarm, Hebron and Bethlehem. The Bank of Palestine was opened in Gaza in 1981; it now has branches in Gaza, Khan Yunis, and Jebalia.

In addition to the commercial banks, various other institutions provide financial services to the inhabitants of the territories: moneychangers, commercial banks in Jordan, commercial banks in Israel, and some non-bank intermediaries in the territories.

Regulatory arrangements for the Cairo-Amman Bank may provide some useful precedents for the transition period. Only Jordanian residents of the West Bank can open accounts and take loans—in either dinars or shekels—with the Bank. Israeli settlers cannot use Jordanian banks. The Bank is supervised jointly but independently by the Central Bank of Jordan and the Bank of Israel. All dinar transactions are supervised by the Bank of Jordan, while transactions in shekels and other currencies are supervised by the Bank of Israel.

Working Assumptions

In considering the development of the monetary and financial systems during the period of transition, we made the following assumptions: the shekel and the dinar will continue as legal tender on the West Bank, and the shekel in Gaza strip during the transition period; no new currency will be introduced during the early stages of the transition; a Palestinian Interim Monetary and Financial Authority (PIMFA) will be set up to pursue the goals of financial sector development in the Occupied Territories; and the central banks of Jordan and Israel will continue to be involved in bank supervision and the formulation of financial policies in the territories.

We recommend that the dinar become legal tender in Gaza, and take it for granted that the extent of financial intermediation has to be expanded.

During the transition period in which the shekel and dinar continue to be the medium of exchange, the capital controls of Israel and Jordan will have to apply to transactions carried out in the respective currencies. Israeli restrictions, which are tighter than those of Jordan, are being relaxed gradually. It would be desirable for Israel to reduce controls further, at least to the point where they are no more restrictive than those of Jordan. All three economies would benefit from the free flow of capital.

Tasks of the Palestinian Interim Monetary and Financial Authority (PIMFA)

The primary mission of the PIMFA will be to help improve the financial system in the Palestinian entity, and thereby contribute to its economic development. A separate agency is needed both because some of its tasks, such as bank supervision, require spe-

Table 1.2
Functions of the Palestinian Interim Monetary and Financial Authority (PIMFA)

1. Chartering, supervision and regulation of new banks in the territories, as well as supervision and regulation of existing commercial banks in the territories.

2. Chartering and supervision of non-bank financial intermediaries.

3. Collection and publication of data on the financial system; and advising the interim self-government on macro-economic policy.

4. Shared responsibility for the creation and operation of necessary public sector financial institutions and intermediaries, such as a development bank (if such institutions are created.)

cialized knowledge, and to ensure that a single institution is charged with this important responsibility.

The initial responsibilities of the PIMFA would be as set out in Table 1.2. Depending on the overall progress of the transition process, the PIMFA could begin to exercise more functions as the transition proceeds. The first two functions would be undertaken in collaboration with the central banks of Israel and Jordan.

We briefly review these functions. First, as the transition gets under way, it is likely both that existing banks will want to set up new branches in the West Bank and Gaza, and that new banks will want to open. PIMFA should certainly regard the opening of more banks in the West Bank and Gaza as a major operational goal. It should be the chartering authority for the new banks and the regulatory authority that grants permission for the opening of new branches.

It should also exercise prudential regulation over the banks. Since both existing and new banks during the transition process will be issuing either shekel or dinar deposits, both the Bank of Israel and the Bank of Jordan will have to take part in the regulatory process. In this way the regulatory and supervisory experience of the two central banks could be transferred to the staff of the PIMFA.

In many countries specialized private institutions finance particular types of activity—for instance, building societies finance home purchases. In other countries universal banks, which provide essentially all financial services, dominate the financial system. Given the small size of the economy of the Occupied Territories, a system with *universal banks*, which provide a very broad range of financial services, would probably be preferable.

Even with universal banking, other financial institutions, such as insurance companies and pension funds, will be needed in the Palestinian entity. PIMFA should be the regulatory and licensing authority for these institutions. Representatives of the regulatory authorities for this type of institution in Israel and Jordan should be members of the PIMFA regulatory committee for the relevant institutions.

The third function, the collection and publication of data on the financial system, derives from PIMFA's regulatory role. The range of information typically published in industrialized countries can be discerned from the *Bulletin* of any of the major central banks, such as the Bundesbank, Federal Reserve, or Bank of England. The PIMFA also should have a policy research group which offers economic advice to the self-governing authority on macro-economic policy.

We include the fourth function although we are not sure that the self-governing authority will set up public financial institutions. Many developing countries have set up public-sector development banks, to finance either development projects or special sectors of the economy. For instance, a development bank may provide special financing for agricultural sector investments, or it may finance infrastructure projects with the assistance of external aid. The overall record of such banks is not very successful, and given the potential for private financing in the West Bank and Gaza, we recommend against the creation of such a bank. But if any such institution is set up, PIMFA should share responsibility for its management.

Many countries have in the past operated postal savings systems, and many still do. In this system, individuals hold accounts in saving banks set up within post offices. The postal savings bank typically invests all its assets in government bonds, and remits the interest to depositors. Since its deposits are covered fully by government bonds, they are effectively insured. The postal savings system in Japan is still the largest deposit-taking institution in the country, and deploys its assets in directions favored by the government. Postal savings systems in Europe and elsewhere also operate a highly efficient giro payments system, whose reach is as wide as the coverage of the postal system.

It appears that the self-governing authority will have control over the postal system during the transition. It would then have to decide whether to set up a postal savings system. The benefits of setting up a postal savings system are that it provides a convenient and widely accessible vehicle for individual saving, that it may provide a large flow of resources to the government, and that it makes it possible to set up an efficient domestic payments system. The disadvantages are that the system competes, often unfairly, with private-sector deposit-taking institutions, and that like the development banks, it may be associated with corruption.

Organization of the PIMFA

PIMFA would be governed by a Board of Directors headed by a Chairman, appointed by the interim government, and including representatives of the central banks of Israel and Jordan. The Board should include representatives of the private sector in the territories, but should be dominated by professionals.

Internally, the PIMFA would be run by a Managing Board, consisting of the Chairman and heads of the main departments. These would include: a banking department, responsible for chartering and supervision of banks; a non-bank financial institutions department; an external economic relations department, responsible for relations with the neighboring central banks, and with operations undertaken by non-Palestinian banks in the territories; and a research department.

The transition process is itself a period of potential change. As the PIMFA gains experience, assisted if possible by technical experts from the international agencies, it would take on more and more responsibility. Looking beyond the transition period, it is possible that the successor institution would want to introduce an independent currency. It would be an easy transition from the arrangements of the PIMFA to a Currency Board, in which the currency is backed fully by foreign assets, to—eventually—a more fiduciary currency.

The Management of Foreign Aid[17]

For the immediate future, foreign financial assistance is likely to be the principal source of funds for public investment in the Palestinian economy, and may also be a source of funding for private investment and public current expenditures. In addition, foreign technical assistance could make an important contribution to the design of economic institutions and the management of the economy during the interim period and later. Foreign assistance therefore has the potential to play a central role in the economic development of the West Bank and Gaza.

---

17. This summarizes the material in Chapter 7.

The Organization of Foreign Aid

Given the likely importance of foreign aid to the economy, and the multiplicity of likely aid donors and agencies, high priority will have to be given to the management of aid. The tasks of aid management include: the preparation of aid requests, based on the priorities of the interim self-government, determined in consultation with all the economic departments; negotiation of aid agreements with donors; overall management of the financing and the execution of projects; and the coordination of the activities of the donors, to ensure that they do not operate at cross purposes with each other and with the development goals of the Palestinians.

All these functions fall under the broad heading of liaison between Palestinian economic decision-makers and the officials of the different aid agencies. We describe these activities as aid coordination, though they should be understood as going well beyond coordination. The aid coordination function should be located in the Department of Finance.

An important part of the aid coordination task is quite mechanical. Aid agencies have various procedures that must be followed before a grant is made. Most aid agencies only adjust country priorities once every two years or longer and, to influence these priorities, one must be prepared to make one's case at these specific times. One of the aid coordinator's roles is to keep track of all of these procedures and timetables and to advise policy-makers as to what they need to do and when they need to do it.

At a more substantive level, aid coordinators need to understand the thinking of the various aid agencies and their resident representatives. They also need to know the priorities of their own leaders. The coordinator's role is then to try to bring these different viewpoints closer together so that decisions in support of development can be made.

Given that aid is already flowing to Palestinians in the West Bank and Gaza, consideration should be given to setting up an aid coordination agency even before the functional equivalent of a department of finance is established.

Aid Objectives and Instruments

International agreement on the importance of peace in the Middle East and the development of a new Palestinian entity should make foreign governments and international organizations willing to provide financial aid to the self-governing authority, on a scale that is significant relative to the size of the economy. Indeed, the volume of aid to the Palestinians is already significant.

The role of foreign aid will be large and diverse, particularly in the early years while a governing structure is being created and the private sector is being revitalized. Several different types of aid will be needed:

1. Project aid: Aid designated to support specific projects will be a major feature of assistance to the West Bank and Gaza for the indefinite future. The priority areas for West Bank and Gaza project assistance include: infrastructure projects; funds to support training and education; funds to support foreign technical assistance; and funds to support welfare programs for low income people.

2. General program aid: Program aid is general non-project financing, to fund the public sector budget, and for balance of payments support. It is quite likely that the revenues of the self-governing authority from taxation and other sources in the West Bank and Gaza, and from agreed transfers from the Israeli government, will fall short of projected expenditures, at least in the early years. Foreign aid may be needed to close the budget gap,

as well as any balance of payments financing gap that emerges once the development plans of the self-governing authority have been specified.

3. Regional projects: Foreign aid can play an essential role in the development of regional projects that involve several countries in the region. Given the small size of many states in the region and the vital role of such joint resources as water and transport facilities, regional infrastructure projects will be essential if these resources are to be used efficiently. Regional projects will also be important vehicles through which the people in the region can learn to work together for constructive ends. External aid funding will often be an essential incentive to bring such projects into being.

The Role of External Organizations

During the transition period, and probably for several years thereafter, the self-governing authority is unlikely to have all the experience and skills required for the tasks it faces. Some of this experience gap can be filled by *technical assistance*, through small teams of individuals working on contract with the West Bank and Gaza economics departments and especially the foreign aid coordination agency. In addition, some Palestinians who have gained experience abroad, for instance in international agencies, are likely to be available to aid the development effort.

Technical assistance in setting up the institutions of economic management would best be provided by the international agencies most experienced at doing so. For instance, the IMF has extensive international experience in the design of fiscal systems and central banks; the World Bank has assisted in the reform and design of financial systems all over the world. The EC has also been active in providing technical assistance in Eastern Europe and the former Soviet Union.

The Role of the IFIs

We share the consensus view that a major financial institution should be involved in the economic development of the West Bank and Gaza, and of the entire Middle East, in conjunction with the peace process. What is needed for the Territories is an institution which will 1) make an appropriate assessment for the donors, and in conjunction with the Palestinian aid coordination agency, of the development needs and priorities within the West Bank and Gaza; 2) set up a framework to coordinate donor assistance, in conjunction with the Palestinian aid agency; 3) help manage general and project aid to the West Bank and Gaza; and 4) provide technical assistance to the self-governing authority. In addition to coordinating assistance from donors, the agency might, if legal conditions permitted, also lend directly to the self-governing authority.

The leading international financial institution, the World Bank, is the natural and appropriate institution to take on these responsibilities. It has vast experience in dealing fairly with conflicting parties. It has begun to play an active role in the multilateral talks between Israel and the Arab countries and is prepared to continue in that role as long as it is desired by all sides. Further, the World Bank is capable of mobilizing the best expertise both from the region and around the world.

As long as the self-governing authority lacks sovereignty, it cannot become a regular member of the Bretton Woods institutions. However, it should not be beyond the abilities of the international community to enable the international financial institutions (IFIs) to provide technical assistance to the West Bank and Gaza, and to coordinate financial assistance from other donors. For instance, special trust funds could be set up to finance technical assistance, and to pay the costs of World Bank (and, where appropriate, IMF) staff involved in the planning and coordination of the overall aid effort.

We have already discussed our recommendation that a regional development bank, the Middle Eastern Bank for Cooperation and Development (MEBCD), be set up. We emphasize again the main rationale for its creation: that because it would emphasize and encourage functional cooperation among the residents of the countries of the region, such a Bank would have a different role than the World Bank.

A Think-Tank

Whether or not a new regional bank is formed soon, there is also a role for a think-tank with experts from both inside and outside the Palestinian entity to provide counsel in the development of the economic plans for the area in general and the Territories in particular. Such a think-tank would be led from the outset by development specialists from the West Bank and Gaza, but its staff could include expatriate specialists particularly in the early years. Such a think-tank would be primarily responsible for providing in-depth analysis and a long term perspective to the policy and planning efforts of those managing aid and development expenditures on a daily basis. This think-tank would complement, not compete with, the more regional perspective of analysts in the proposed regional bank.

Appendix A

Work on this project began in Cairo, Egypt on January 7, 1992 with a meeting of a small group of Israeli, Jordanian, and Palestinian economists. The result of the meeting was a plan of work for the project. That plan is described briefly here.

The economists meeting in Cairo decided that the project would be about the economics of the five year period of Palestinian self-government. This meant the development of broad policy recommendations regarding Palestinian economic relationships with Israel and Jordan; and, to a lesser extent, the Palestinian economy itself. While the economists from Harvard and MIT, as well as the staff of the Institute, were reticent about intruding into what could be considered the province solely of Palestinian economists, the economists and staff were encouraged by the latter at a meeting in Jerusalem on January 10, 1992 to cover in this project a broad range of subjects in economics that could be of great interest to Palestinian policy-makers— even subjects pertaining to matters of a purely Palestinian nature.

Both in Cairo and, two days later, in Jerusalem, the economists agreed on working in five areas: the institutions of the interim self-governing authority for the management of the Palestinian economy; fiscal matters; international trade; the financial sector; and foreign aid. At a later stage, the area of labor was added. The understanding was that in each of the six areas the principal concern was Palestinian economic relationships with Israel and Jordan.

Thereafter, the project entailed separate meetings of each of the six groups. Each of the economists within the groups had the task of preparing materials, by themselves or in pairs, for an eventual single paper that represented both the prepared materials and the views of the economists in each of the six groups.

A senior economics professor from Harvard or MIT chaired each group. He first solicited ideas on topics from the members of his group; prepared a memorandum in which he gave his group its "charge"; and then convened at Harvard a meeting of his group. These initial meetings generally lasted one and a half days, and yielded a deeper understanding of the task of the group as well as an assignment of responsibilities for the preparation of written materials on an agreed list of subjects. Upon submission by the several Israeli, Jordanian and Palestinian economists of their materials, the six group chairs proceeded to draft for the first time a single paper for the group.

In late February, 1993 the "steering committee" for the project convened at Harvard. This committee was composed of four Israeli, four Jordanian, and four Palestinian economists, and was chaired by two of the Harvard-MIT economists. At this February meeting, the members of the steering committee evaluated the six draft papers and discussed them in some detail with each of the six group chairs. This led to a re-drafting of the six papers. The editorial committee that was established by the steering committee reviewed the summary paper. The process was concluded in June, 1993.

2   Agriculture, Industry, Services, and Trade

Raymond Vernon, *Chair;* Omar M. Abdel-Raziq,
Hisham Awartani, Ahmad Qassem El-Ahmad,
Abdel Rahman Al-Fataftah, Michael Michaely,
Mahmoud K. Okasha, Ezra Sadan.
Other Contributors: Gideon Fishelson, Hind Salman

By international standards, Israel, Jordan, and the West Bank and Gaza are each very small entities with limited internal markets. Their capacity for economic growth will depend on a heavy continued commitment to international trade and international investment; in the absence of such a commitment, their opportunities for growth will be greatly limited. Given the geographical propinquity of the three areas under consideration, one would normally expect to see this commitment expressed in growing trade and investment among them. The recommendations below are directed to a considerable degree at facilitating such possibilities during the transition, while taking into account the acute differences in the starting conditions of the different parties.

Starting Conditions

The differences in the starting circumstances of the parties is striking in a number of different respects, as can be seen in Table 2.1. To begin with, in 1991, Israel's gross national product of $59 billion was about fifteen times that of Jordan, and Jordan's

Table 2.1
Selected Economic Characteristics of Israel, Jordan, and the West Bank and Gaza[a]

	Israel	Jordan[b]	Occupied Territories W. Bank	Gaza	Combined
GDP (mil $)	59127	4083	1668	560	2228
GNP (mil $)	58989	3764	2134	864	2998
GDP per capita ($)	11962	1050	1700	850	1350
GNP per capita ($)	11878	968	2175	1310	1800
GDP by sector (%):					
Agriculture	2.4	8.3			20.6
Industry	21.8	26.5[c]			7.3
Construction	10.2				
Services	65.6	65.2			72.1[c]
Exports/GNP	30.6	29.8	10.5	13.3	11.3
Imports/GNP	46.2	66.2	29.3	34.8	30.9
Population (mil)	5.06	4.14	1.01[d]	0.68	1.69[d]

a. Figures for Israel and Jordan are for 1991. Total and per capita GNP and GDP figures for the Occupied Territories are averages of 1990 and 1991 figures.
b. Jordan's income for 1991 was low as a result of the Gulf War. In 1990, GDP per capita was $1340.
c. Includes construction.
d. Does not include East Jerusalem.

Sources: Data on Israel and West Bank and Gaza are from Central Bureau of Statistics, *Statistical Abstract of Israel*, 1992; Jordanian data are from Central Bank of Jordan, *Monthly Statistical Bulletin* (Vol. 28, No. 12, December 1992).

Table 2.2
Other Economic Characteristics of Israel, Jordan, and the West Bank and Gaza[a]

	Israel	Jordan	Occupied Territories W. Bank	Gaza	Combined
GNP/GDP (%)	99.8	92.2	127.9	154.3	134.5
Labor Participation Rate (%)	36.0	17.5			17.0
Population under 15 (%)	30.4	44.0			48.8
Consumption/GNP (%)[b]	62.0	127.3	72.9	70.7	72.3
Investment/GNP (%)[b]	24.0	23.0	21.9	21.2	21.7
Gov. Spend. (%)[b]	30.0	28.0	7.9	7.9	7.9

a. Unless otherwise noted, all figures are for 1991.
b. Data for West Bank are for 1987, data for Gaza are for 1990.

Sources: Labor force data are from Chapter 3, Table 3.1. All other data are from *Statistical Abstract of Israel*, and Central Bank of Jordan: *Monthly Statistical Bulletin*.

GNP was larger than that of the West Bank and Gaza.[1] Correspondingly, the per capita GNP of Israel is substantially higher than that of Jordan and of the West Bank and Gaza. Israel's per capita GNP for 1991 was roughly $11,900 while Jordan's was $1,000[2] and that for the West Bank and Gaza was $1,800.[3]

As Table 2.2 demonstrates, the differences in the structures of the three economies are also very marked, reflecting very different patterns of development in recent decades. There is a substantial difference between GDP and GNP in the West Bank and Gaza, with GNP exceeding GDP by an average of one-third. This difference primarily reflects the Palestinians' heavy dependence on the Israeli labor market for employment[4] in addition to private remittances from abroad. Labor force participation rates are significantly lower in Jordan and the Occupied Territories than in Israel. As Chapter 3 discusses, the entire region suffers from an overall underutilization of labor. In Jordan and the Occupied Territories, this is reflected in low participation rates, part-time employment, and high unemployment, while in Israel, the low utilization is reflected primarily in high unemployment. Table 2.2 also shows a substantially younger population in Jordan and the Occupied Territories than in Israel, which explains some of the differences in participation rates. Public sector spending is also much lower in the Occupied Territories.[5]

Economic relations among Israel, Jordan, and the West Bank and Gaza have been strikingly unbalanced. Under the terms of the Arab boycott, Jordan does not trade with Israel. The West Bank and Gaza, on the other hand, have been heavily dependent

---

1. Data for Israel and Jordan are from the *World Bank Atlas, 1992*; for the West Bank and Gaza, estimates are based on data in the *Statistical Abstract of Israel*.
2. Per capita GNP in Jordan in 1991 was low as a result of the Gulf War; the estimate for 1990 was $1340.
3. Average for 1991.
4. Labor market issues are discussed in more detail in Chapter 3.
5. Fiscal issues are discussed in Chapter 5.

on the economy of Israel for markets and sources of supply, while their trade with the much smaller economy of Jordan has been modest. During the years in which data were available, the West Bank and Gaza succeeded in achieving a small positive merchandise trade balance with Jordan while sustaining a large negative balance with Israel. This negative merchandise trade balance with Israel was to a considerable extent offset by trade in services, consisting mainly of labor exports from the West Bank and Gaza to Israel. These labor flows help tie the West Bank and Gaza closely to the Israeli economy.

Before the onset of the Intifada in 1988, according to some estimates, almost 40 percent of the labor force of the West Bank and Gaza (some 110,000 workers) were employed in Israel, a figure that is reported to have dropped slightly to about 34 percent since. Accordingly, about one third of the GNP of the West Bank and Gaza depends upon their transactions with Israel, whereas less than 5 percent of Israel's GNP is attributable to its links with the West Bank and Gaza.[6] While Israel's overall economic dependence on the Occupied Territories therefore is small, both Israeli agriculture and construction have been heavily dependent on labor from the territories.

The differences in the structures of the three economies and the asymmetry in their patterns of dependence clearly have not been due to economic forces alone. Jordan's participation in the Arab economic boycott of Israel accounts in part for the limited relations of Jordan to the other parties. And the extent of the dependence of the West Bank and Gaza on the economy of Israel is explained in part by Israel's control over the trade of those areas and by Israel's use of workers from those areas in its labor market.

---

6. The 5 percent number is an attempt to take into account both direct Israeli exports to the Territories, and the fact that Palestinian labor in Israel has been about 100,000 people, while the number of Israelis in the labor force is about 700,000.

Although it is evident that a period of closer cooperation among the parties can benefit them all, one of the paramount aims of leaders in the West Bank and Gaza will be to expand their contacts with other economies beyond Israel and Jordan, identifying other markets and other sources of supply, and eventually reducing the degree of their dependence on their immediate neighbors. Israel, too, will wish to reduce the dependence it has shown in some sectors, such as construction, for labor from the West Bank and Gaza. Any program for enhanced cooperation among the various parties will have to take cognizance of these objectives.

The introduction of a period of close cooperation among the three entities will present initial problems not only for the West Bank and Gaza but for Israel and Jordan as well. Each of them has to deal with pockets of protection in their respective economies that will feel threatened by the new era of cooperation. In Israel, protection is concentrated in the agricultural sector, for example, in dairy products, poultry, and vegetables. Also, water is subsidized in various locations. Jordan, too, protects agriculture and industry.

History tells us, nonetheless, that problems such as these can be overcome. The extraordinary developments in Europe over the past forty years, which have brought the economies of France and Germany together in an association that very few could foresee, is striking evidence of the possibilities for change in international relationships. Successful associations such as the European Community have usually taken cognizance of a limited number of cases meriting special treatment, without allowing such exceptional cases to swamp the movement toward greater cooperation among neighboring countries. The recommendations below, therefore, point in a general direction, rather than providing a detailed prescription for change.

Basic Principles for Trade and Investment

The basic objective governing our recommendations is to promote the growth of Israel, Jordan, the West Bank and Gaza, applying policies that take due cognizance of the differences in the starting positions of the various parties. In particular, we will focus on the potential for economic development in the West Bank and Gaza, the area which will experience most economic change in the event of peace.

In framing our recommendations, we have drawn on the experience of developing countries all over the world during the past four or five decades. These affirm that there is a major place for government in any development strategy—but that the more successful strategies of governments are those that make extensive use of the market, restraining the urge to target individual industries and individual firms for selective treatment. National and international measures to build infrastructure, improve human resources through training and education, encourage entrepreneurship, promote technological development, mobilize capital, and facilitate a search for markets, play a vital role in any development strategy. Measures to restrict investment and trade, on the other hand, run the substantial risk of generating unintended consequences harmful to the development process.

With regard to economic relations among the three entities, our basic proposal is for Israel, Jordan, and the West Bank and Gaza to pursue coordinated policies in the transitional stage that are consistent with eventually achieving a free trade area in goods, services, capital, technology and in due course, labor. Insofar as obstacles exist to that goal, they presently take the form of measures imposed by Israel and Jordan. In terms of lifting existing restrictions, therefore, our proposals would place the principal obligations on Israel and Jordan, requiring only restraint from the West Bank and Gaza.

To achieve their objectives of growth and to develop a wider network of relationships at the same time, the West Bank and Gaza would avoid the use of restrictions and prohibitions on trade, employing positive measures of support for their people and their enterprises in order to promote their objectives. Included among such supportive measures would be the mobilization of foreign sources of private and public capital, as well as the negotiation of trade and investment agreements with foreign countries.

We recognize that many in the West Bank and Gaza will be strongly tempted to use import restrictions and other restrictive economic measures as a means of reducing their dependence on the economy of Israel. But the experience of small developing countries over the past few decades speaks so eloquently for the destructiveness of restrictive economic measures that we see the decision of the West Bank and Gaza to avoid such restrictions as critical for their well being.

Our first recommendation is that Jordan, Israel, and the West Bank and Gaza should work towards free trade among them. Given the current lack of trade between Israel and Jordan, this process may have to proceed by aiming initially for two free trade areas, one between Jordan and the Occupied Territories, and another between Israel and the Territories. Current arrangements between Israel and the West Bank and Gaza embody a large measure of free trade, and it should be relatively easier to move towards free trade in this area.

The creation of a free trade area between Jordan and the West Bank and Gaza would, at least with respect to the West Bank, restore a situation that existed before 1967. But given the starting point of very little trade, such an arrangement would take some time to implement. At the same time, free trade could be developing between Israel and Jordan. This preference for early action, even if it requires a double bilateral approach, applies to all of the recommendations that are offered below.

To implement these suggestions, Israel, Jordan, and the West Bank and Gaza should as soon as possible launch a series of discussions aimed at defining the free trade area objective, shaping the content and duration of the interim steps toward that objective, and structuring the institutions needed for the execution of such plans.

The economic development of the West Bank and Gaza will in addition benefit from increased trade with countries other than Jordan and Israel, and provision will have to be made for the West Bank and Gaza to set up trade relations with countries other than Jordan and Israel. It is quite likely that the European Community will be willing to grant favored access to goods from the Territories, and that possibility should be vigorously pursued. New arrangements will also have to be made for the import and export of goods to and from the West Bank and Gaza, requiring both agreements about customs treatment and perhaps special port and airport arrangements.

Agriculture

The Present Situation

The agricultural sector is of greater importance to the economies of Jordan and the West Bank and Gaza than to Israel, even though agriculture carries considerable political and ideological weight in Israel. As Table 2.1 shows, the agricultural sector in Israel accounts for only 2.4 percent of GDP. It represents about the same percentage of its exports, and employs a little over 4 percent of its labor force. Although the trade policies of Israel have in general created a relatively open economy in that country, the agricultural sector is for the most part under the tight control of official marketing boards, being strongly protected from foreign competition, and receiving extensive support in technology and planning from government agencies. Recently some agricultural marketing boards have been abolished, and it is likely that the agricultural sector will have to depend more on markets than it has hitherto. Our recommendations, if put into effect, would lead to a further significant freeing up of the restrictions under which this sector operates, a trend welcomed by a considerable part of the sector itself.

In Jordan, agriculture plays a significantly larger role in the economy, representing about 8 percent of GDP and 15 percent of the country's exports. As in Israel, the sector enjoys a high level of import protection. Although the technological and marketing support that Jordanian agriculture receives from the government is less substantial than in Israel, Jordan feels that its agricultural sector offers considerable promise for the future.

Agriculture has been of critical importance to the economies of the West Bank and Gaza, with the West Bank heavily committed to the production of olives and Gaza to citrus fruit. As Table 2-1 indicates, the agricultural sector contributes about 21 percent to the GDP of the West Bank and Gaza, with substantial variations from one year to the next mainly due to variations in the value of the olive crop. Agriculture accounts for 27 percent of the labor force and for 19 percent of the exports of these areas.

Unlike Israel and Jordan, however, the agriculture of the West Bank and Gaza has not been protected from competition with their neighbors. While Palestinian agriculture received significant support from the Israeli agricultural extension service in the period after 1967, there has not, in the 1980s, been much direct governmental support, either in technology or in marketing. Restrictions on water use, inferior support services, and restrictions imposed by the Israeli military on exports to Israel have had the effect of limiting the possibilities of raising the productivity and increasing the market opportunities of producers in these areas.

Positive elements stimulating agricultural production in the West Bank and Gaza have been the proximity of the Israeli and Jordanian markets plus some support early in the occupation period from Israel's agricultural extension services. Some products not produced in adequate quantities by Israeli producers have been admitted to Israel, while others have been moved clandestinely into Israeli markets in arrangements often developed jointly with Israeli distributors. Jordan, too, has allowed the importation of some goods in these categories, enough to generate a negative trade balance with the West Bank and Gaza.

Despite these exceptions, however, the agricultural sectors of the West Bank and Gaza have been unable to contribute much to the growth of the economy. Agriculture grew at an annual rate of 8.6 percent for the period 1972–79, during the first decade of the occupation period. The performance during the 1980s was much weaker, however. There appears to be considerable room for expansion of this sector, particularly its exports, as the West Bank and Gaza gain self-government.

The agriculture of the West Bank and Gaza is complementary in considerable degree to that of Israel. Competition is to be found in vegetables, citrus fruit, and poultry production. But Israel enjoys advantages at the present time in livestock, various types of non-citrus fruits, annual crops such as flowers and cereals, breeder poultry, and processed agricultural products. The West Bank and Gaza maintain an advantage in sheep and goats, olives and figs, and vegetables requiring intensive labor inputs such as tomatoes, cucumbers, squash, and possibly potatoes.

Future Policies

The long term objective in agriculture among Israel, Jordan, and the West Bank and Gaza should be that of free trade. Even if the West Bank and Gaza continue to place considerable importance on the objective of reducing their dependence on the Israeli market, that objective would not be served by encouraging a regime of protection. Indeed, given that agriculture is likely to be an area in which the West Bank and Gaza have a comparative advantage (provided water is not subsidized in Israel), the West Bank and Gaza would benefit in this area from reciprocal and substantially free trading arrangements. The political pressures to protect agriculture are more likely to be greater in Israel and Jordan, but protectionist policies will prove increasingly unwise for all the parties over the longer term. One reason stems from mounting costs of corruption and enforcement. The length of the borders among the parties and the difficult terrain through which these borders pass encourage large scale smuggling, a situation already apparent in various poultry and vegetable markets today. Moreover, with increasing growth in the area, each of the parties has a growing need for resources available in greater abundance in one of the other countries—the West Bank, Gaza, and Jordan for the technology, market contacts, and capital available in Israel,[7] and Israel for the supply of agricultural labor available in the West Bank and Gaza. That situation suggests, in fact, that freer trade in the region would encourage complementary rather than competing agricultural activities, at least until the time that incomes in the territories of the various parties approach common levels.

Our basic recommendation in the area of agriculture is that Israel, Jordan and the West Bank and Gaza move gradually towards free trade among them. In this area, too, it may be simpler to proceed through a series of bilateral agreements than by attempting to reach an initial overall agreement among the three entities.

---

7. Israeli agricultural technology, especially in irrigation, is recognized to be of very high quality. This is one of the few non-oil sectors in which Israeli-Egyptian trade is important.

We emphasize that an agreement to move toward a free trade goal in agricultural products cannot mean instantaneous transition from a state of restricted trade to one of open borders. After a long history of protection in the agricultural sectors of both Israel and Jordan, interim arrangements involving a gradual phasing out of trade restrictions and subsidies would be indispensable.

The West Bank and Gaza will also want to develop direct agricultural links with other economies. Both the Gulf countries and Europe could provide markets for high quality Palestinian agricultural exports.

The development of West Bank and Gaza agriculture will require cooperation with the neighboring economies in a wide range of areas, most critically water rights. To achieve that cooperation, it will be necessary to deal with some deep-seated conflicts and grievances in a fair and effective manner.

Progress in that direction will demand, among other things, that the water authorities in each of the areas begin pricing that commodity in a closer relationship to its real market value. Once the issue of water distribution is effectively addressed, the parties will be in a far better position to improve their use of the existing water resources of the region and to mobilize international efforts for the purpose of increasing total supply. In any event, the movement toward a free trade regime in agriculture must be accompanied by a rationalization of water use.[8] While it is commonly asserted that the water problem faces overwhelming difficulties, we believe that the declining importance of agriculture in the Israeli economy, along with the accompanying gradual move towards higher water prices for Israeli agriculture, will make it possible to solve the problem. With a fair agreement on water use in hand, authorities in the West Bank and Gaza will

---

8. This is a subject addressed by another working group, which is not producing a paper for this report.

be able to proceed to develop irrigation schemes for agriculture. For this purpose it should be able to draw on both Israeli and Jordanian expertise, and that of the international institutions. The effective use of irrigation will require the provision of power to the agricultural sector. In addition, agricultural development in the West Bank and Gaza will require improved transportation, storage, and other infrastructure and credit facilities.

The creation of transportation infrastructure within the West Bank and Gaza will be the responsibility of the self-governing authorities in those areas, while facilities for transporting exports will have to be designed in collaboration with the neighboring economies. We anticipate that credit facilities for agriculture will be provided by the private banking system that should develop in the territories. Worldwide, the experience with special agricultural and land banks has rarely been favorable, and we do not recommend the creation of a special bank for agricultural credit. Similarly, the creation of storage facilities can usually be left to the private sector.

Agricultural research and extension has played a key role in increasing productivity, and research should be directed to the special needs of Palestinian agriculture. There would be many advantages to the creation of an agricultural research center in the West Bank and Gaza. It would be natural and desirable for such an institution to work in close collaboration with agricultural research facilities in Israel and Jordan, and also to draw on international expertise.

As has already been noted, the West Bank and Gaza will need technical and financial support for putting in place a number of programs indispensable for effective performance in agricultural markets. Much of this support will come from outside sources, including multilateral development banks, non-governmental organizations, and governments. In some areas, however, such as in the control of animal and plant diseases, close cooperation among Israel, Jordan, and the West Bank and Gaza will be indispensable.

Accordingly, we recommend also a series of measures aimed at the development of agriculture in the West Bank and Gaza. These include:

• An agreement on the use of water;

• Improved credit facilities for agriculture, which we expect to be provided largely by the private sector;

• Improved infrastructure for transportation, irrigation, and power, which will require actions primarily by the self-governing authority and also by the neighboring governments;

• The strengthening of institutions for research in the technology of agriculture and agro-industries—an area where indigenous research capacity in the West Bank and Gaza should be developed, and where international cooperation can also play an important role;

• Improved control of animal and plant diseases, which will require close cooperation with neighboring economies.

To help achieve these ends, a high level committee composed of representatives of the parties should jointly map out the steps for the promotion of free agricultural trade among the three entities, as well as other resources where joint action among the entities is needed.

The action program would not be complete if it did not address the relationship of the free trade regime to the marketing boards, subsidy schemes, product standards, and other national measures maintained by Israel and Jordan. In addition, the self-governing authority will want to reach agreements with other countries willing to provide market access for Palestinian agriculture or to provide technical assistance for agricultural development in the West Bank and Gaza.

Industry

The Present Situation

As with agriculture, the industrial sectors of Israel, Jordan, and the West Bank and Gaza are in strikingly different states of development. Israel has developed a relatively modern industrial sector, with a considerable technological capacity, a substantial reliance on capital markets, and a heavy reliance on exports. All told, the industrial sector generates about 22 percent of the country's GDP, but over 90 percent of the country's merchandise exports.

Israel's industry operates with very little protection in world markets, being a signatory to various trade agreements that commit it to a reduction in import barriers on industrial goods, including a free trade agreement with the United States, various accords with the European Community and the members of the European Free Trade Area, and membership in the General Agreement on Tariffs and Trade.

Jordan includes an industrial sector characterized on the whole by smaller plants with a lower level of technology and a higher degree of family ownership and financing. The industrial sector (including construction) accounts for about 27 percent of the GDP and 47 percent of exports. Manufacturing makes up half of the industrial sector, comprising about 14 percent of GDP. Existing import barriers for industrial goods basically take the form of tariffs, with rates varying from 30 percent to as high as 150 percent (e.g. luxury cars).[9]

Industrial establishments account for about 9 percent of the labor force working in the West Bank and 14 percent of the labor force working in Gaza. Although there have been a few striking

---

9. Figures on Jordan are from the Central Bank of Jordan's *Monthly Statistical Bulletin*, Vol. 28, No. 12, December 1992. Figures are for 1991.

cases of enterprises in the West Bank and Gaza that have incorporated sophisticated industrial techniques and have competed successfully with Israeli industrial enterprises, most of the manufacturing establishments of the West Bank and Gaza have been small in size, approximating cottage industries. Of the 3700 industrial establishments reported in the West Bank and Gaza in 1991, as Table 2.3 shows, fewer than 300 reported more than 10 workers. Not surprisingly, therefore, the typical enterprise is family-owned and family-managed, with capital resources coming from inside the family; indeed, less than 10 percent of total industrial investment in the West Bank and Gaza comes from commercial banks or other visible financial intermediaries.

The data in Tables 2.3 and 2.4 show the dominance of very small enterprises in the West Bank and Gaza. The data also reflect the reliance of industrial producers in the West Bank and Gaza on the Israeli economy: four out of every ten industrial workers are employed in the production of textiles, clothing, and leather products, industries composed largely of subcontractors to Israeli enterprises.

It is common for small economies to rely on subcontracting of this kind in early stages of industrial development, and some of the existing activities would be expected to continue in the West Bank and Gaza so long as the economies of the region remain open to one another.

The possibility of improving the capabilities and productivity of the industrial sector of the West Bank and Gaza has been blocked by various conditions, some associated directly with the occupation and some stemming from other causes. Among the military policies that have been reported as blocking the opportunities for the development of the industrial sector in the West Bank and Gaza are:

• A licensing policy that discouraged the establishment of large industrial enterprises (abandoned as of the beginning of 1991, according to Israel);

Table 2.3
Industrial Establishments in the West Bank and Gaza in 1991; by Employed Persons and Major Branch

Major branch	West Bank				
	1-3	*4-10*	*11-20*	*21+*	*Total*
Food, beverage & tobacco	18	171	12	11	244
Textiles, clothing & leather products	215	119	45	28	406
Wood and its products	303	52	3	1	359
Metallic industries	401	90	8	8	507
Other industries	291	134	35	34	464
Total	**1228**	**566**	**103**	**82**	**1979**
Major branch	Gaza				
	1-3	*4-10*	*11-20*	*21+*	*Total*
Food, beverage & tobacco	75	33	3	5	116
Textiles, clothing & leather products	245	273	45	8	570
Wood and its products	259	55	4	4	322
Metallic industries	314	60	2	3	378
Other industries	215	93	17	1	325
Total	**1106**	**503**	**71**	**21**	**1710**

Source: C.B.S. (1992); *Statistical Abstract of Israel*, Jerusalem.

Table 2.4
Contribution of the Industrial Sector in the West Bank and Gaza to Employment, by Major Branch in 1991

Major branch	West Bank		Gaza	
	employment	*%*	*employment*	*%*
Food, beverage & tobacco	2351	20.7	583	8.2
Textiles, clothing & leather prod.	2758	24.4	2969	42.2
Wood and its products	864	7.6	1056	15.0
Metallic industries	1465	12.9	1163	16.5
Other industries	3899	34.4	1269	18.1
Total	**11337**	**100.0**	**7039**	**100.0**
As percent of total labor force	—	6.3	—	6.5
As percent of total locally employed	—	9.2	—	10.7

Source: C.B.S. (1992); *Statistical Abstract of Israel*, Jerusalem.

- Military restraints on the movement of materials into and out of the territories;
- Limited local banking for the financing of local industry;
- Restraints on the development of free trade zones, other industrial zones, and related infrastructure;
- Restraints on the development of supporting public institutions.

These policies have exacerbated the problems of the area that in any case would have existed, such as the limited size of the local market, the poverty of its inhabitants, and the lack of training and experience of its people in industry. The policies of Jordan in maintaining tight controls over West Bank exports, as well as the uncertainties over access for Palestinian products to the Israeli market, have added still further to the area's difficulties.

Future Policies

In the industrial sector, Israel, Jordan, and the West Bank and Gaza have no choice but to rely heavily on imports and exports as a basis for development. Each of these areas provides a domestic market so small as to rule out a strategy of import substitution as a serious basis for an industrial take-off. Besides, the record of small countries pursuing an import-substitution strategy over the past few decades indicates the high risks and substantial limitations of such a strategy.

With import substitution ruled out as a serious possibility for a take-off strategy, development policy will have to rely on an export-oriented strategy. Such a strategy would have two essential components: first, improving the access of the West Bank and Gaza to the markets of other countries; and, second, improving the capacity of producers in the West Bank and Gaza to exploit the opportunities of such improved access.

At the present time, however, the West Bank and Gaza suffer from severe handicaps relative to their neighbors in the industrial sector, lacking capital, technology, and managerial skills. The few striking successes among entrepreneurs in these areas that already have taken place suggest that the potential for industrialization in the area is considerable.

It can be anticipated, however, that if the West Bank and Gaza are granted improved access to other markets including Israel and Jordan, the firms in the best position to exploit the new possibilities will sometimes be foreign-owned. In the past, governments in many developing countries placed severe restrictions on foreign direct investors; but in recent years, few governments have continued such restrictive policies. Many have succeeded in capturing positive externalities from the existence of foreign-owned firms, over and above the contributions of such firms in the form of jobs and taxes. By providing encouragement to foreign-owned enterprises to conduct training programs and create indigenous sources of supply, for instance, governments have commonly added to the positive results of such investment.

Such results have demanded, however, that indigenous entrepreneurship and training should be strongly supported and encouraged at the same time. They have required governments to use considerable restraint and selectivity in applying their powers to screen and condition foreign investments. Such forbearance may prove especially difficult for the West Bank and Gaza, whose industrial possibilities have for so long been dominated by the industrial sector of Israel; but any strongly restrictive policy on the part of the authorities in these areas will place a heavy cost on the development of the areas.

We recommend an export-oriented strategy for the industrial development of the West Bank and Gaza, which would involve:

- developing agreements with governments within and outside the region that would remove the obstacles to the flow of capital

and technology across borders in the region, including agreements covering the rights and obligations of foreign investors
and agreements that would enlarge the market opportunities of
the West Bank and Gaza;

- supporting the indigenous private sector in its efforts to mobilize capital, technology, infrastructure, and training required for
modern industry; and in its efforts to find markets abroad;

- encouraging foreign direct investors to contribute to these
objectives

Presumably, any agreements among Israel, Jordan, and the
West Bank and Gaza governing the conduct of the parties in
trade and investment will be asymmetrical in the early years,
allowing greater tolerance for government sponsored promotional measures on the part of the West Bank and Gaza than for
their more developed partners in such agreements. Such tolerance would be particularly important as long as the West Bank
and Gaza did not have the option of devaluing a national currency. Such asymmetries are typical of international agreements
among countries at different stages of development, as can be
seen in the provisions of the General Agreement on Tariffs and
Trade and in the agreements between the members of the
European Community and the so-called ACP countries of
Africa, the Caribbean, and the Pacific.

A word of caution is necessary, however. The evidence suggests that countries exploiting such a preferential right do not
always benefit thereby. This adds to the importance of recognizing firmly from the very first that the ultimate goal should be
achieving the elimination of border restrictions on the flow of
capital, goods, and technology in the industrial sector.

Services

It is increasingly being recognized that the transborder flow of
services represents a critical part of the international interaction

required for the successful development of industry and trade. In the case of Israel, Jordan, and the West Bank and Gaza, the services that will prove of immediate interest in an era of self-government are tourist services, transportation (including especially airports and buses), electric power, and banking; eventually, some of the licensed professions, such as engineers, physicians, and accountants, may be added to the list. These activities are also of importance because some of them offer special opportunities for direct collaboration among the parties in the region. Tourist services offer a particularly strong challenge because of the potential importance of that sector to an autonomous West Bank and Gaza. Although successful collaboration in tourism will depend fundamentally on enterprises in the private sector, governmental agreements to facilitate transportation and border crossings will also play a significant role. There is also room in this area for collaboration with Egypt.

Some problems in the provision of services across borders will require especially urgent attention during the transition. With self-government, the West Bank and Gaza will be presented with some immediate problems in transportation that are readily foreseen. One such problem relates to the availability of an airport, presumably involving the formulation of terms on which Palestinians can avail themselves of the international airports of Israel and Jordan. Other problems relate to bus routes and schedules, and the planning of roads. The development of a multinational electric power grid offers added opportunities, especially for markets as small as those represented by Israel, Jordan, and the West Bank and Gaza.

Many service activities, however, are the subject of some unique regime of national regulation. Accordingly, the objective of encouraging movements across international borders in a given field usually presents some problems distinctive to the particular field.

Each regulated service area in which constructive cooperation seems possible should be taken up in a committee of experts, with the object of producing realistic programs for cooperation among the parties. We recommend therefore, that working parties of experts, operating under a strong mandate to reduce national barriers to transborder movements, should be appointed in the following areas: tourist services, airport and seaport facilities, bus facilities, road and bridge facilities, and electric power.

We present recommendations regarding financial services elsewhere. And at some appropriate time in the future, it will prove useful to create working parties similar to those proposed above for each of the licensed professions, with a mandate for reducing or eliminating barriers to the transborder sale of services.

Conclusion

As the prospects increase for the creation of an interim self-government regime in the West Bank and Gaza, thoughtful leaders will have to confront the problem of reconciling a number of conflicting objectives: How to seize the opportunity for improving the lot of all the people in the region through cooperative measures; how to provide more effectively for the deficiencies of the West Bank and Gaza arising out of decades of war, occupation, and resistance; yet how, at the same time, to make provision for the desire of the West Bank and Gaza to reduce the degree of their dependence on Israel and Jordan induced by these abnormal conditions.

To achieve these goals, we have recommended an aggressive economic strategy for the West Bank and Gaza, aimed at promoting the development of these areas through open markets and the expansion of exports. Our recommendations have been framed at two different levels. First, we have proposed that the West Bank and Gaza pursue a set of broad relationships with countries in the region, especially with Israel and Jordan, based on the principles of a free trade area, through a series of bilateral agreements if necessary. Second, we have proposed a series of more specific practical measures in the fields of agriculture, industry, and services, aimed at increasing the effectiveness of the West Bank and Gaza in its participation in the world economy. Together, these measures should add greatly to the future prospects of the West Bank and Gaza as well as for its relations with other countries in the region during the period of transition.

3

Palestinian-Israeli-
Jordanian Labor Mobility:
The Current Situation
and Issues for a Peaceful
Future

Richard B. Freeman, *Chair;* Abdelfattah Abu-Shokor,
Ahmad Qassem El-Ahmad, Ruth Klinov

Introduction

In the area of labor flows, maintenance of the *status quo* would
make an important contribution to peace and stability. Israel
should not sharply reduce the employment of Palestinians in
Israel. Jordan cannot absorb a large increase in the flow of
Palestinian workers from the Occupied Territories of the West
Bank and Gaza.

These conclusions result from observing the high rates of
labor underutilization in the Jordanian and Palestinian
economies, coupled with the awareness that time is needed to
create the large number of new jobs every year that both
economies need. To open the Jordanian labor market to a sizeable number of Palestinian workers and the Palestinian labor
market to a large number of Palestinian workers compelled to
leave the Israeli labor market would create, in the short-run,
greater unemployment, poverty, and political radicalization
both in Jordan and the Occupied Territories.

Current labor market policies among Israel, the Occupied
Territories of the West Bank and Gaza, and Jordan derive in part
from the fact that the three are contiguous areas with relatively

Table 3.1
Population and Labor Force: Israel, Jordan and the Occupied Territories (1991)

Country	Population ('000) (yearly average)	Labor Force ('000)	Labor Force/ Population (%)
Israel	4,946.3	1,770.3	36
Jordan	3,453[a]	700[a]	175
	3,888[b]	645[c]	
Occupied Territories [exc. Jewish settlers*]			
Total	**1,640.7**	**312.1**	**19**
West Bank	981.3	200.3	20
Gaza	659.4	111.8	17
Total	**10,475.0**	**2,634.4**	**25**

a. Estimate reported in Dr. Gil Feiler, Prof. Gideon Fishelson, and Dr. Roby Nathanson, "Labor Force and Employment in Egypt, Syria and Jordan", discussion paper for the Histadrut-General Federation of Labor in Israel, Institute for Economic and Social Research series on The Impact of Regional Developments on the Middle Eastern Labor Market, April 1993.
b. Estimate reported in Dr. Ahmad Qassem El-Ahmad, "Jordanian Labor Market", mimeo, Royal Scientific Society, March 1993.
c. 553,000 reported labor force in sectoral distribution blown up on the basis of estimated unemployment of 14.4% (from Dr. Ahmad Qassem "Jordanian Labor Market" and revisions to same).
*Jewish settlers [000']: 94.1. West Bank: 90.3; Gaza: 3.8

Sources: Israel and Occupied Territories: Israel, Central Bureau of Statistics, *Statistical Abstract of Israel 1992*, table 2.1, 12.1, 27.1, 27.18. ; Jordan: El-Ahmad, Ahmad Qassem, *The Jordanian Labor Market*, p. 7, table 2. and Feiler, Fishelson and Nathanson, p. 48 and p. 54, tables 3 and 4.

small populations and labor forces (see Table 3.1). The distances between the areas are small, so that commuter migration has been a major form of labor mobility between Israel and the Occupied Territories, and could be a major form of mobility between Jordan and the other two entities.

Patterns of labor mobility have been determined not only by economic forces, such as the large differences in factor endowments, but by political barriers to development. These barriers, in turn, have contributed to a rather slow increase in employment and production in the Occupied Territories, as well as to a situation in which a high proportion of the Palestinian labor force—34 percent in 1991—are employed in Israel.[1]

The three areas under discussion have different factor ratios, which implies that each would benefit from close economic ties. The capital-labor ratio in the Occupied Territories is about one-fourth that in Israel. The difference in labor productivity are similar: GDP per worker in the Occupied Territories appears to be on the order of 27 percent of GDP per worker in Israel.[2] The West Bank and Gaza and Jordan have less educated work forces than that of Israel. Half of Jordan's work force is employed in the public sector, while much of the Palestinian work force is employed in agriculture or construction, both in Israel and the Territories.

As the overall report argues, these three areas (and others in the Middle East) should cooperate in a common trading, investment, and work area. This would benefit all three economies, although, during the transition to open borders, some factors of production would lose in each of the entities. But even though high labor mobility will benefit the economies involved, it is already clear that there are strong pressures to reduce Palestinian employment in Israel. High unemployment, social friction, security considerations and political difficulties would continue to produce such pressures. On both the Israeli and Palestinian sides, there is now a preference for shifting employment of Palestinians from Israel to the Territories. Jordan would seek to avoid a substantial inflow of Palestinian workers.

---

1. Details in Table 3.2.
2. This estimate is of the same magnitude as pay differentials between Israelis and Palestinians. In 1990, gross wages per employee-post of Palestinian workers employed legally in Israel were 22 percent those of Israelis. Moreover, gross wages of domestically employed Palestinian workers are lower than those of Palestinian workers in Israel. Angrist [1992] finds that between 1987 and 1989 Palestinian domestic workers earned about 80 percent of net wages earned by comparable Palestinian workers working in Israel. The combined effect is to make Palestinian domestic wages about 18 percent that of Israeli labor.

While we accept the inevitability of these trends, it is important to caution against radical cuts in Palestinian employment in
Israel: the benefit to both sides from its continuation is evident
from the fact that even after the curtailment of such employment
in the Spring of 1993, it is still substantial. Also, the expected rate
of expansion of jobs in the Territories in the near future calls for
a gradual rather than abrupt relocation of Palestinian labor. In
time, Jordan's history of exporting high skill and importing low
skill labor argues for a more open policy in the future.

This chapter discusses labor market issues for the next few
years. Section II sketches the recent labor market situation in all
three entities, focusing on the range of expected employment
growth of Palestinians inside the Territories, and the implica-
tions for their future employment in Israel. Section III describes
the present institutions governing the employment of
Palestinian workers in Israel. Section IV addresses the issue of
policy measures aimed at expanding Palestinian employment
and production within the Territories themselves. The discussion
overlaps other papers in this report, and is, therefore, kept brief.
Section V summarizes the regulation of wages and fringe benefits in the three areas, addresses the question of the treatment of
social insurance contributions made in Israel by Palestinian
workers, and offers options for dealing with the problem.
Sections VI deals with the treatment of Palestinians by trade
unions in Israel and the Territories.

The Labor Situation: Underutilization and Mobility

Relocation of labor, as well as reforms in labor market institutions, should be put in the context of the increasing overt and
hidden underutilization of labor in all three countries. The conjunction of the Gulf crisis, the Intifada, and Soviet migration to
Israel have considerably raised unemployment, part-time

Table 3.2
Unemployment, Part-Time Employment, and Absenteeism (Percent of the Labor Force in 1980, 1987 and 1991)

Country	Date	Unemployment	Part-Time Employment	Absenteeism	Total
Israel	1980	4.82	4.0	8.9	37.7
	1987	6.12	6.4	8.5	41.0
	1991	10.6	25.1	7.8	43.5
WestBank	1980	1.5	7.4	3.9	12.8
	1987	2.5	4.1	2.8	9.4
	1991	10.3	10.7	4.3	25.3
Gaza	1980	0.4	2.5	4.1	7.0
	1987	1.6	3.2	5.9	10.7
	1991	4.1	7.7	7.5	19.3
Jordan	1986	8.0			8.0
	1989	10.3			10.3
	1991[a]	19			19

Sources:
Israel, Central Bureau of Statistics: *Statistical Abstract of Israel 1992*, table 12.1, table 27.18.
El-Ahmad, Ahmad Qassem: *The Jordanian Labor Market*, mimeo, March 1993, p.3.
a. The RSS in Jordan, conducting a household survey in mid-1991, reached a somewhat lower estimate—14.4%.

employment, and absenteeism from work (see Table 3.2). It is clear that improving labor market performance requires an increase in employment in the region as a whole. Also, in all three labor markets, rules set for employment of migrant labor are expected to be sensitive to the high domestic unemployment. In Israel, underutilizatiom of labor is best captured by overt unemployment, which increased between 1980 and 1992 from 4.8 to 11 percent of the labor force.[3]

In contrast, in the Occupied Territories, underutilization is mostly captured by part-time employment and absenteeism, which reflect a combination of a recession and the frequent work

---

3. Changes in part-time work reflect the increasing participation of women rather than involuntary reductions of labor inputs; absenteeism reflects mostly changes in army reserve service.

interruptions due to the Intifada. In the West Bank the total of
the three components rose sharply between 1980 and 1991, from
12.8 to 25.3 percent, and in Gaza from 9.0 to 19.3 percent.[4] Jordan reports a rise in its unemployment from 4.3 percent in 1982
to 19 percent in 1991.[5] Jordan's population grew by roughly 10
percent after the Gulf War, increasing the unemployment rate by
6 to 7 percentage points and costing the economy massive remittances. Since the more educated were over-represented among
immigrants, the return flow also has increased the human capital of the work force.

Palestinians depend heavily on the Israeli labor market for
employment, especially after the closure of employment opportunities in the Gulf States and Jordan that had existed prior to
the Gulf War (see Table 3.3). About one-third of the labor force in
the Occupied Territories was employed in Israel in 1991. This is
an average between the West Bank [31 percent] and Gaza [39
percent]. Despite the drop of 5-6 percentage points from the pre-
Intifada situation, the figures indicate heavy dependence on
Israel. The construction industry is the chief employer of these
workers: it employs 68 percent of the Palestinians who work in
Israel and 23 percent of the entire Palestinian labor force. Some
of these workers are skilled, but most are semi-skilled or
unskilled, as are the majority of Palestinian workers in other
Israeli sectors. Agriculture employs 12 percent of the
Palestinians who work in Israel.

---

4. There are conflicting estimates of the rate of unemployment among Palestinians.
Israel's Central Bureau of Statistics data gives estimates of 10.4 percent and 4.1 percent for the West Bank and Gaza respectively in 1991, but some claim that these
estimates are too low. Farris, Fishelson, Jubran, and Nahanson (FFJN) cite figures
from an independent survey of Palestinian university college graduates that shows
higher rates of unemployment than do official statistics for that group. In addition,
there is low participation of older, less skilled Palestinian males in the work force,
due in part to their losing ground in unskilled work to younger men.
5. Dr. Ahmad Qassem El-Ahmad, "Jordanian Labour Market," Royal Scientific
Society, Amman, Jordan, March 1993, p. 3.

Table 3.3
Number of Persons Employed in the West Bank and Israel by Region of Residence and of
Employment, 1970–1991 (Thousands)

	West Bank			Gaza			Israel		
	Total	Employed:		Total	Employed:		Total	Reside:	
		locally	in Israel		locally	in Israel		locally	outside
1970	114.6	99.8	14.7	58.7	52.9	5.9	983.8	963.2	20.6
1975	132.3	91.9	40.4	72.5	46.7	25.9	1178.9	1112.6	66.3
1980	134.8	94.3	40.6	80.9	46.3	34.5	1329.6	1254.5	75.1
1985	151.2	103.8	47.5	90.6	48.9	41.7	1457.5	1368.3	89.2
1986	167.0	115.7	51.3	94.1	50.7	43.4	1462.6	1367.9	94.7
1987	177.6	114.7	62.9	100.1	54.1	46.0	1512.6	1403.7	108.9
1988	183.0	119.0	64.0	98.9	53.5	45.4	1562.5	1453.1	109.4
1989	180.8	115.4	65.4	98.7	59.2	39.5	1565.7	1460.8	104.9
1990	192.6	128.0	64.6	103.9	60.8	43.1	1599.6	1491.9	107.7
1991	179.7	123.8	55.9	107.7	65.9	41.8	1,680.8	1583.1	97.7

Source: Kleiman, updated from Appendix to 1992 article.

The larger size of the Israeli population makes Israel propor-
tionately less dependent on Palestinian workers than
Palestinians are on jobs in Israel. Palestinians constitute some 6
percent of the Israeli work force, but are largely employed in
low-level laborer-type jobs so that their share of labor's contribution to the economy is less than 6 percent. The Israeli government has committed itself to reducing the number of
Palestinians in Israel, though this will be a difficult process. It
will require growth of demand for labor in the Occupied
Territories as well as reductions in demand for Palestinians in
the Israeli economy.

There are several reasons for expecting a decline in Israeli
demand for Palestinian workers in the near future:

• The increasing psychological and monetary cost of day-to-day
friction between commuting Palestinians and Israelis;

• Stronger competition from Israeli immigrants and others
among the unemployed: even though most Russian immigrants
to Israel are skilled or professional, at the first stages of their
absorption they often compete for jobs traditionally filled by

Palestinian workers. Also, the protracted rise in unemployment of non-immigrants may induce some of the unemployed to enter jobs they previously refused;

• Declining profits by employers: Israeli employers may find the employment of Palestinians less profitable, if they face stronger competition (and thus higher wages) for Palestinian labor from Palestinian employers; and

• The decline in demand for construction: the recent construction boom is largely over, and is not expected to repeat itself in the near future, unless a new mass wave of immigrants arrives.

A decline in Palestinian labor supply to Israel may also be expected, insofar as the domestic demand for labor in the West Bank and Gaza increases. Any steps toward self-government will create public-sector demand for white collar professional and administrative workers, many of whom are presently employed as semi-skilled laborers in Israel (many others are fully or partly unemployed). Deregulation of credit, investment, and trade, and thus an increase in these activities, are expected to increase labor demand in the private sector in the Territories. The extent of the resulting decline in Palestinian employment in Israel and the rise in domestic employment cannot be forecast accurately. Key issues include: What will be the investment and employment response to the lifting of present barriers to trade, investment and financing in the West Bank and Gaza? What will be the size of the public sector? What additional labor will be supplied by returning Palestinian refugees? The latter will be an outcome of an agreement in the peace talks.

The Institutional Setting for Labor Mobility

In the ensuing discussion of the institutional framework for the employment of Palestinians in Israel, a major consideration is the rise in the share of illegal workers, to which the rules

Table 3.4
Legal Territories' Workers' Posts and the Annual Value of 5 Percent Tax Deduction, 1975–1990 (In 1989 Dollars)

Year	Posts-Average per Month (000')	Percent of Legal out of Total Employed in Israel*	Annual Wage Bill of Legal Workers in 1989 Dollars (000')	5 percent Deduction in 1989 Dollars (000')	Gross Annual Wage per Post (1989 Dollars)
1975	47.9	72.2	180,000	9,000	3758
1980	43.7	58.2	187,560	9,378	4292
1985	39.8	44.6	157,920	7,896	3968
1986	41.5	43.8	205,440	10,272	4950
1987	47.2	43.3	270,720	13,536	5735
1988	44.4	40.4	257,520	12,876	5800
1989	36.3	34.6	215,400	10,770	5934
1990	35.6	33.0	215,300	10,765	6048
1991	62.0	64.4	282,410	14,120	4555**

*Legal *posts* from National Insurance sources divided by number of *employed* in Israel derived from Labor Force Surveys.
**The low earning per post reflects a drop in the number of days worked per average post, and possibly also a decline in real wages.

Source: Israel Central Bureau of Statistics: *Statistical Abstract of Israel 1992*, table 12.32, table 27.23.

described below do *not* apply. The percentage of legal out of total Palestinian workers in Israel[6] declined from 71 in 1973 to 33 in 1990 (see Table 3.4), with the main motivation being avoidance of taxes and National Insurance contributions, as well as paying wages below the mandatory minimum level. But since the Gulf War, and particularly in the first nine months of 1992, there has been a turnabout, and the percentage rose to 65. This was achieved by facilitating compliance by employers through computerization of the system and also through stricter enforcement of the rules. Once political separation takes place between Israel and a Palestinian entity, enforcement will probably be easier; and, this fact, coupled with recent administrative

6. Estimated by the ratio of Palestinians employed in jobs as reported by the National Insurance Institute (NI) to the total number of Palestinians employed in Israel, as reported in labor force surveys.

improvements, leads one to believe that future coverage will be nearer to two-thirds rather that a third.

Procedures for recruiting Palestinian workers are coordinated with those for recruiting Israeli workers, of which we give a brief description here. Under the Employment Service Act, Israelis, except those in professions and higher managerial positions, are required, on accepting a job, to register in a Ministry of Labor exchange office (LEO) in their area of residence. Registration is employer-specific, and change of employer requires a new registration. Independent of that, and subject to the National Insurance Act and ordinances, employees must report to the National Insurance Institute (NI) on each new worker and pay the mandatory contributions on the worker's behalf. There is no evidence about the extent of compliance with the Employment Service Act, but it seems that the NI coverage of the Israeli labor force is virtually complete.[7]

The rules for recruiting Palestinian workers date to a 1972 Military Ordinance, "General Exit Permit," which has been revised several times, the latest being on June 1, 1992. The following description applies until now. Palestinians are required to carry a work permit. Persons employing Palestinians without a permit are fined, and their workers are detained. The recruitment procedure is for employers to apply to the labor exchange office in the district in which work is to be carried out in order to be issued a permit, given after the LEO has posted the vacancies for two weeks, and after no Israeli job applicant has applied for the job. The permit is addressed to the LEO district payment-office, through whom the employers signs an agreement to make all his/her payments (wages, NI deductions and fringe benefits). In fact, employers make advance payments directly to their workers and report them to the payment office, which pays the

---

7. According to Labor Force Surveys, the number of Israeli employees in 1991 was, 1,288,600. The NI counts the number of employee jobs, rather than that of persons, and, due to multiple job holding, the number reported for 1991 is 1,770,300.

workers any residuals. Upon signing the agreement, the employer is issued an authorization to apply to a LEO in the Territories.

Workers residing in the Gaza Strip who wish to work in Israel need, in addition to the labor exchange permit, a permit to enter Israel, which is required of all Gaza residents, workers and non-workers. These are magnetic cards, distributed by the Civil Administration on the basis of security considerations, and are limited to persons aged 25 and older. West Bank residents who had at any time been detained on security grounds also require a special entry permit. Under no conditions are Palestinian workers allowed to stay the night in Israel. Their daily transportation is the responsibility of their employers.

In Jordan, Palestinians, including those with Jordanian passports, are treated as are all other foreign workers in that they are not allowed to reside in Jordan or work there without a work permit. The Ministry of Labor in Jordan estimates that 26 percent of the total labor force in 1991 consisted of foreigners (legal as well as illegal). Most imported labor works in agriculture, services and construction. Ninety-six percent of permit holders in 1991 were blue collar workers, mostly employed in agriculture and services; and a sizeable number were part of foreign construction crews. At the same time, Jordan has traditionally exported skilled labor: 280,000 Jordanians worked overseas in 1992.[8]

Developing Palestinian Employment in the Occupied Territories

Both the Israelis and Palestinians would like a shift in Palestinian employment from Israel to the Occupied Territories, and some such shift may already be underway. But the numbers

---

8. Qassem, March 1993, Table 1, p. 4.

are such that *continued large-scale employment in Israel* is likely to be a major element for the Palestinians in the foreseeable future, if widespread unemployment and poverty are to be avoided. Ignoring the return of Palestinians presently living in other countries into the Territories, and assuming the Palestinian labor force increases at the 1980-1987 rate, the annual addition to labor supply will be on the order of 9000.[9] For these workers to find employment in the domestic Palestinian labor market, i.e., in the West Bank and Gaza, the annual rate of growth of employment would have to more than double from the present level of 4,000.[10]

In view of the level of employment of Palestinians in Israel (roughly 110,000 prior to the curtailment in the spring of 1993), supplying jobs in the Territories for all those currently employed in Israel within a five year period would involve the need for another 20,000 annual new jobs, thus a total of 29,000. If the number of returnees to the Territories during a five-year period is sizeable, this would add to the difficulty of absorbing both growth in the Palestinian labor force and creating new jobs in the Palestinian entity to scale down the employment of Palestinians in Israel.

The bottom line has two parts: one is that while the objective of supplying jobs in the West Bank and Gaza to the additional labor force seems feasible, a sizable decline in the existing stock of Palestinian workers in Israel could cause widespread unemployment. In particular, continued employment in Israel of 100,000 Palestinian workers is required. It seems reasonable to expect a continuation of the employment in Israel of a substantial number of Palestinians from the Territories.

---

9. Estimates of annual Palestinian labor force increases are based on Table 3-3. ILO (1991, p. 11) estimates are higher, 12,000 persons.
10. E. Kleiman, "Flow of Labor Sources from the West Bank and Gaza to Israel." Working Paper #260, Department of Economics, Hebrew University, July 1992, Appendix.

Another part of the bottom line is that avoidance of ethnic friction demands the creation of jobs at an accelerated rate in the West Bank and Gaza. This means taxes have to be kept to a minimum, as do regulations constraining business. Free trade and the free flow of capital will provide the stimulus for efficiency and thus competitiveness. Foreign aid, as noted in the chapter on this subject, has to be channeled away from human services and towards creating conditions for job creation in the private sector. The activities of the proposed regional development bank also have to be brought to bear on the task of creating private sector jobs.

Continued large-scale commuter migration from the Palestinian entity to Israel would require agreements on labor mobility between any new Palestinian entity and Israel. Policies regarding the general population movement, such as the requisite magnetic card in Gaza, are motivated by security considerations and could potentially be relieved by the peace process. Israel will have to decide on the allowable amount of illegal labor, weighing various factors (the costs of enforcement of the law, the reduction in Palestinian employment, and the effect of stricter enforcement on the wages and fringe benefits of Palestinian workers.) Regarding the recruitment procedures, Israel is likely to continue to give priority to Israeli unskilled and semi-skilled workers during the transition period, though this policy does not seem to have been particularly effective.[11]

---

11. For example, up to 1991, the efforts of employment exchanges to secure more jobs for Israelis at the expense of Palestinian workers were unsuccessful. This can be tested in the following way: the expected policy of labor exchanges would be to change the number of Palestinian work permits issued by the employment service, inversely to changes in the number of Israeli job applicants. Correlation analysis corroborates this, but further testing reveals that the negative correlation is totally washed out by the increase in illegal Palestinian employment: as Israeli unemployment goes up, legal Palestinian employment declines, but this decline is more than offset by the increase in illegal Palestinian employment. As a result, the priority-to-Israelis policy secured them better jobs than those assigned to Palestinians, rather than a larger amount of jobs.

Even though Jordan cannot, at present, absorb additions to its heavily unemployed labor force, some contribution may be made in areas in which it already employs foreign labor, mainly in construction. If Palestinian construction companies entered into agreements with Jordan, this could provide a source in Jordan of new jobs for workers in the Occupied Territories.

In view of the possibility that inter-country labor mobility will increase in the more distant future, it would be advisable to initiate an effort to standardize occupational licensing, to exchange students in vocational training programs, and to be liberal in granting companies the permission to open branches in each other's countries.

Regulation of Wages and Fringe Benefits

The Israeli and Jordanian labor markets are highly regulated regarding hours of work, vacation, safety and wage-setting. Jordanian labor law limits hours worked; provides a three month probation period for new employees; requires notification of layoffs by one week to one month, or severance pay; sets a minimum wage; and requires contributions for national insurance and social security. Workers have both injury and occupational health insurance and invalidity, old age, and death insurance. The employer contributes 2 percent of monthly wages for the former and 8 percent of monthly wages for the latter benefit. An additional 5 percent is deducted from the workers' pay. The law requires that private employers give a 14-day paid annual leave and up to 14 days of sick pay.

The Israeli labor market is highly regulated regarding hours of work, vacation, safety, etc. Severance pay on termination of work, at the rate of one month per year of employment, is mandatory in all cases where job duration is above one year. Industry-based pension funds cover a high percentage of employees. Last, most workers pay insurance premiums for medical services provided by one of the non-profit organizations, the largest of which, Kupat Holim, belongs to the General Federation of Labor, the Histadrut.

Because Palestinians are less educated and younger on average than Israelis, they earn considerably less in the Israeli labor market. However, Kleiman estimates that the wage differences between "comparable" Israeli and Palestinian workers in Israel (those who are the same age, have the same schooling, etc.) are on the order of 20 percent.[12] This does not, however, mean that Palestinians do not face any discrimination in the Israeli job market, for instance in access to better jobs.

Israeli regulations and collective agreements provide sizeable benefits for Palestinians that account for a substantial proportion of labor costs. Palestinians have the right to most of the benefits accruing to Israeli workers, which are obtained through collective agreements between the Histadrut and the employers union in the relevant sector. Employer and employee deductions for these benefits are apparently at the same rate as those of Israeli workers. Benefits are paid partly by the LEO payments offices, and partly by employers. These benefits, which are not part of the National Insurance system, include: paid annual leave, paid sick leave, family medical insurance, and retirement pensions. Severance pay for layoffs is paid only by the construction industry. Additional benefits vary by industry and include bonuses for length of service, invalidity and survivors' pensions. Employee deductions for these benefits amount to 5.5 to 6 percent of gross salaries, and employers' contributions vary widely: 37.3 percent in construction, 19.5 percent in agriculture, 12.5 percent in other sectors. The extent to which Palestinians actually use the different benefits is, however, unclear.

---

12. Kleiman, Working Paper #260, July 1992.

A major issue regarding the Palestinian workers in Israel is that they are excluded from many of the benefits provided by National Insurance for Israeli workers. While Palestinians hired through employment offices pay social insurance taxes, they do not receive commensurate benefits. Palestinian workers are eligible for National Insurance [NI] benefits in the event of work-related accidents, maternity [in the unlikely event that birth takes place in Israel], and insurance of severance pay in case of employers' bankruptcy. They are not entitled to child allowances, unemployment insurance, and old-age pensions.

Since their NI contributions are at the same rate as those of Israeli workers, Palestinians have put more into the system than they have received in benefits. There are competing estimates of the magnitude of this differential. To get some sense of the amounts involved, Table 3.5 reports National Insurance date on deductions and benefits in Israel, from the US Department of Health and Human Services [1990]. The table shows that total deductions without eligibility for benefits are 8.55 percent of gross earnings, with employees paying 4.5 percent, and employers 4.05 percent.[13]

Table 3.4 estimates the annual sum, in 1989 dollars, of a 5 percent tax deduction, which is the number used here to estimate *employee* contributions in excess of their benefits. It shows contributions in excess of eligibility to benefits in the range of $10 million a year.[14] It ignores employer contributions for which workers received no benefits based on the notion that this in fact

---

13. ILO (1992, p. 30) reaches a similar estimate for employees—4.3 percent, but a higher one—6.88 for employers.
14. The calculation was done as follows: the total gross wage bill of Territories' workers from which taxes are deducted (i.e. legal work) is obtained as the difference between the total (Israeli plus Territories) and the Israeli gross wage bill in current shekels, as reported by the National Insurance Institute. This was then deflated by the consumer price index for 1989=100, and converted by the average 1989 exchange rate (NIS/$ = 1.9182) to dollars. All data are from the CBS *Annual Statistical Abstract*.

Table 3.5
Benefits, Tax Rates and Qualifying Conditions

Type of Program	Coverage of Palestinians	Source of Funds— Percent of Gross Earnings	Qualifying Conditions
old age, invalidity, death, and long term care.	no	employees 4.35 employers 1.95 government 0.95	age 65—men: age 60—women; 5 years insurance in last 10 years, or total 10 years insurance
sickness and maternity	yes	employees 0.6 employers 0.1	maternity benefits —10 months of insurance in last 14 months, or 15 in last 22 months
work injury	yes	employees 0.55 employers 0.55	no minimum qualifying period
unemployment	no	employees 0.15 employers 0.1	180 days of contribution out of 360 days worked, or 270 days out of 540 worked
family allowances	no	employees none employers 2.0	children under 18
total deductions with elegibility		employees 1.30 employers 0.75	
total deduction		employees 4.5 employers 4.05	

Source: US Department of Health and Human Services: *Social Security Programs Around the World - 1989*, Research Report #62, SS publication No. 13-11805, May 1990.

was a wage equalization tax whose incidence fell on employers and ultimately, on Israeli consumers.[15] This leaves an order of magnitude of nearly 250 million dollars as the maximum difference between employees' contributions and benefits, cumulated, ignoring interest, over the past 25 years.

---

15. Angrist (1993) finds a high supply elasticity of Palestinian workers to Israel, leading to the conclusion that the incidence of payroll taxes was mostly on employers.

The Israeli government states that a substantial part of this sum was remitted to the budgets of the Civil Administration (spent on setting up a health and social service system in the Occupied Territories, etc.), and thus should be deducted from the balance. But these figures have never been published. Such a remittance treats social security contributions as taxes rather than as insurance. If they are viewed as taxes rather than as insurance payments by workers, the issue becomes one of weighing *overall* taxes paid (in Israel) versus benefits received (in the Territories), and thus, there need not be a separate NI accounting.

To the extent that some of the past balances are recognized as insurance over-payments by Palestinians working in Israel, the amounts due to them could either be transferred in their name to a Palestinian social insurance fund, if it is established; or paid to them in cash; or granted to them in the form of retroactive insurance rights in Israel; or a combination of the three. Similar options are open for the future: namely, to establish a Palestinian social insurance fund—a provident fund is suggested below— to which monies currently paid by employers would be given in the name of each worker; to credit Palestinian workers with the contributions in the Israeli social insurance system, or to reduce their contributions. If, on the other hand, past balances are treated as taxes, they could be designated for a general purpose, or provide the initial funding for a Palestinian social insurance fund.

Three NI benefits do not accrue to Palestinian employees at present: child allowance, unemployment benefits, and old-age pensions. The first two are tied to one's residence rather than to one's work location, and possibly will not accrue to Palestinian workers in the future as well. Old age benefit is a borderline case. If Palestinians are eligible for pensions, they should make contributions; if they are ineligible, they should not. A very important issue is the continuity of health insurance and other fringe benefits for persons working intermittently in Israel and in the Territories. Two possibilities include:

• Palestinian workers leaving Israeli employment but wishing to maintain continuity of health insurance will be charged a higher premium than Israeli workers, covering the contribution made by the employer [as is paid by the Israeli self-employed]; and, to the extent the services are subsidized by the government, the subsidy;
• Palestinian workers employed in Israel will be allowed membership in a Palestinian medical-service fund, should one be established, and their deductions for health would go directly to this fund.

We recommend some consideration by the Palestinian self-governing authority and its Department of Finance of establishing a Palestinian "provident fund," as exists in Singapore. Under the provident fund system, individuals receive benefits strictly in accord with their contributions: benefits received are a function of contributions and interest on invested contributions. There are no interpersonal transfers.

Two key questions are the types of risks covered by the provident fund and the required level of contributions. Although initially per capita income will be low in the emerging Palestinian entity, we suggest that the fund cover the risks of low income in old age, work-related accident insurance. Consistent with what has been argued in the paper presented in this report by the group on fiscal affairs, benefits in the area ought to be limited so that contributions can be kept at a tolerable level at the outset. As Palestinian per capita income grows, contributions and benefits should be increased. In due course, contributors to the provident fund should be permitted to use a fraction of their personal endowment in the fund to purchase housing and higher education for their children. Again, this assumes growth in per capita incomes and, correspondingly, contribution rates.

A particular advantage of the provident fund is that it encourages personal savings. If rates of return on domestic investment are high, these savings can be channeled into private sector activities that will create domestic jobs for Palestinian workers. But provident funds cannot stand alone. They must be supplemented by social assistance benefits.

Unionization

The labor unions on the West Bank are organized into a federation called the General Labor Unions of the West Bank; there are six unions in the Gaza strip. These unions represent workers in those areas but not in Israel. There is disagreement about the extent to which these unions function as "business unions" as opposed to political organizations. Their activities are restricted to the Occupied Territories.

Although Palestinian workers in Israel are covered by Histadrut collective agreements, they are not members of Histadrut nor represented by that union, although they may be involved in plant-level union activity. That Palestinian workers in Israel have no organization defending their interests is an unusual situation, as foreign workers are recruited by domestic trade unions in most countries.

Jordanian law recognizes trade unions. In 1991 there were 17 recognized labor unions. In addition, Jordan gives the physicians' and engineers' associations control of licensing of those professions. There are licensing of lawyers and mechanics in garages. There are industrial courts to handle labor disputes.

The lack of union representation of Palestinian workers in Israel might be addressed through two strategies: Histradut admitting these workers as regular members, as is the practice for foreign workers in most countries; or recognition by Israeli employers and Histradut of a Palestinian union federation, whose members would have specified rights in the Israeli system. This was the way national unions emerged in the U.S. and other countries from local unions: locals would accept the cards of members of other locals, to whom dues were paid, and agree to represent them. Palestinian participation at the plant level, membership in Palestinian national unions, and coordination between the Israeli and Palestinian national unions, might work best. A specific area in which closer coordination is necessary is the processing of Palestinian workers grievances against Israeli employers. Israeli workers' grievances are taken up at the plant, in a local workers' council [which is a geographically based Histadrut organization], or the union. Representatives of Palestinian unions should participate in resolving matters concerning their members in the appropriate councils and unions.

Conclusion

This chapter has discussed existing and future connections among the Palestinian, Jordanian and Israeli labor markets. We distinguish between the short and the long run: in the long run, regional labor market integration is desirable, and is in line with the traditional high labor mobility in the Middle East. But in the short run, building a strong domestic Palestinian labor market is imperative, with labor mobility to Israel serving as an extremely important safety valve.

Our paper discusses the short run, recognizing the priority of promoting job creation in the Occupied Territories. This requires investment, deregulation, and the overhaul of the tax system. We leave the detailed discussion of these issues to other chapters, but emphasize the importance for the labor market of all growth enhancing policies—increased investment, deregulation,

expansive fiscal and monetary policies. Focusing on fiscal policies that have an impact on the labor market, it is recommended
that in order to make the Occupied Territories competitive in the
market place, payroll taxes and social security contributions be
kept to as moderate a level as is possible.

Even under the most optimistic scenarios, however, full
employment requires that substantial numbers of Palestinians
will continue to work in Israel. Therefore, parallel to expanding
job opportunities for Palestinians in the West Bank and Gaza,
our other main concern is easy transferability of workers' fringe
benefits between the Territories and the Israeli labor market by
making the benefits paid in either market cumulative. This will
enable the phasing out of Palestinian employment in Israel to be
done at low cost to workers and will facilitate smooth mobility
between the markets.

At present Israel is levying from Palestinian workers the same
contributions to Israel's social security network as from Israeli
workers, but granting Palestinian workers less benefits. In the
future, correction should be made partly by reducing Palestinian
workers' contributions and partly by expanding their entitle-
ment to benefits. As to compensation on account of past balances between Palestinian workers' contributions to and benefits
from the Israeli National Insurance system, there are two matters
to be settled: how to calculate the balances, and what the sums
involved are. In this paper we spell out the various positions on
the matter, but do not recommend a specific solution.

Another problem is the lack of due representation of
Palestinian workers at the plant level and in processing grievances at the local council and union level. This should be correct-
ed by guaranteeing equal voting rights at the plant level, and by
having representatives of unions in the Territories participate in
negotiations and grievance processing of their members carried

by the corresponding Israeli union. Such representation is particularly important in construction and agriculture.

In the longer run, Jordan, Egypt, and others, as well as the Palestinian entity, may consider the possibility of forming and joining a common Middle Eastern labor market. A limited start could be made by all countries involved, in view of their considerable use of foreign companies for construction projects, by letting each other's companies compete for contracts. Also, some standardization of occupational licensing and some exchange programs in vocational training may pave the way for greater labor mobility in the future.

References

Abu-Shokor, Abdelfattah. *Palestinian Labor Mobility and Work Conditions.* Jan. 1993, mimeo.

Angrist, J. *Wages and Employment in the West Bank.* Hebrew University, Jerusalem, June 1992, mimeo.

Blampain [1992]: *Labor Law and Industrial Relations of the European Union.* Kluwer Law and Taxation Publishers, Deventer, Boston.

International Encyclopedia for Labor Law and Industrial Relations. (Kluwer).

El-Ahmad, Ahmad Qassem. *The Jordanian Labor Market.* March 1993, mimeo.

Farris, Amin; Gideon Fishelson, Raymond Jubran, Roby Nathanson. *The Labor Market in the Territories.* Histradut General Federation of Labor In Israel Institute for Economic and Social Research Discussion Paper, Tel Aviv, April 1993.

Feiler, Gil; Gideon Fishelson, Roby Nathanson. *Labor Force and Employment in Egypt, Syria, and Jordan.* Histradut General Federation of Labor In Israel Institute for Economic and Social Research Discussion Paper, Tel Aviv, April 1993.

International Labor Office. *Report of the Director General, ILO Conference, 78th session.* Appendices, vol. 2: Report on the Situation of Workers of the Occupied Arab Territories, 1991.

International Labor Office. *Report of the Director General, ILO Conference, 79th session.* Appendices, vol. 2: Report on the Situation of Workers of the Occupied Arab Territories.

Kleiman, E. *The Flow of Labour Services from the West Bank and Gaza to Israel.* Hebrew University, Department of Economics, Working Paper #260, July 1992.

Roy, Jean Louis [1991]: *A Guide to the European Economic Community Charter,* Colliers.

Semyonov M. and Levin-Epstein, N. *Hewers of Wood and Drawers of Water.* Cornell, 1987.

Venturini, Patrick. *1992, The European Social Dimension.* Commission of the European Communities, Document, 1988.

US Department of Health and Human Services. *Social Security Programs Throughout the World - 1989.* Research Report #62, May 1991.

World Bank. *World Development Report 1992. Washington DC,* 1992.

4   Institutional Structure for the Palestinian Economy During the Transition Period

Henry Rosovsky, *Chair;* Jawad Anani, Hisham Awartani, Maher El-Kurd, John D. Montgomery, Don Patinkin, Emanuel Sharon, Mohammed Shtayeh

The report of this group focuses mainly on the process of institution-building during the proposed interim period of self-government. For this period to be productive, an institutional structure must be developed which will facilitate Palestinian management of their economy and the coordination of policies between the Palestinians and their economic partners, Israel and Jordan. A sketch of such a structure is offered below.

Our most important recommendation is that Palestinians should at the outset of the interim period of self-government assume leadership of and utilize the existing institutions of the Israeli Civil Administration for the West Bank and Gaza.

We focus on institution-building during an interim period with the goals of achieving economic sovereignty and economic betterment for the Palestinians living in the Occupied Territories, with significant control of natural resources, taxation, finance and other economic institutions. At the same time, we intend for these changes to entail minimum costs for Israel and Jordan; indeed we believe that the new arrangements will on balance benefit both Israel and Jordan. In what follows, discussion of political choices regarding the interim period and the period that follows is kept to the minimum needed to pursue the matter at hand, i.e., the design of the institutional structure.

The institutions we propose are for the Palestinian Interim Self-Government Authority (PISGA), hereafter referred to only as the "interim self-governing authority," and the land is referred to interchangeably as the "West Bank and Gaza" or the "Occupied Territories."

Terms such as "autonomy" or "self-government" have no precise definition in international law with respect to either the political or economic responsibilities of a governing authority. Historically, "autonomy" has referred to a wide variety of arrangements.[1] While the terms autonomy or self-government clearly relate to the extent of independence or control that a people in an area exercise over their own institutions of governance, they do not imply a specific degree of control, nor do they necessarily suggest the domains in which control is exercised.

Although the institutions that ought to be created during the interim period are not self-evident, we believe that autonomy or self-governance is meaningless without substantial control in particular domains. Indeed, if significant control is not extended to a self-governing authority with regard to natural resources such as water and land and with respect to trade, taxation, and finance, then the political purposes of autonomy—recognition of a distinct people, their separation from others, and ownership rights—cannot be achieved. We should point out that in various autonomies around the world important powers sometimes are shared with neighboring sovereigns. An example involves natural resources such as water, whose sources may span politically accepted boundaries between entities. Such power sharing, which takes place also between countries, would serve to reduce the potential negative impact in certain policy areas resulting from policies of the interim self-governing authority on neighboring Israel and Jordan.

---

1. Historical instances of autonomy characteristically consisted of carefully designed, unique rights assigned to a territory or population. Among these, economic rights have always been among the most precisely defined.

Table 4.1
Structure of the Israeli Civil Administration for the Occupied Territories

Department A	Department B	Department C
Infrastructure	Education	Economy
National Parks	Health	Employment
Public Works	Welfare	Industry and Commerce
Archeology	Justice	Agriculture
Wild Life Reservations	Internal Affairs	Fuel
Custodian of Abandoned Property	Religious Affairs	Insurance
Public Property Assessor	Housing	Statistics
Cartography	Electricity	Tourism
Population Registry	Telecommunications	Mines
	Postal Services	Taxation
	Water Resources	Customs

The types of economic institutions that a Palestinian entity will require are heavily influenced by the economic system which will characterize that economy. As is indicated clearly in the summary chapter for this report, participants assume and recommend that the new entity will have an open, market economy, with a relatively small public sector. Accordingly, the economy will be dominated by private enterprises financed through the private sector and subject to competition from both local and foreign firms.

Institution-Building for the Palestinian Economy

Utilizing Existing Governmental Institutions

Given the immediate economic problems that the Palestinians will face upon assuming primary responsibility for their fate, the most advisable approach to institution-building is to have the interim self-governing authority rapidly assume control of the existing agencies of the current Israeli Civil Administration for the West Bank and Gaza. Other Israeli bodies have jurisdiction as well, with reference to certain activities and to certain geographic areas. In making this central recommendation, we in no way mean to confine the responsibilities of the interim self-governing authority. We intend with this proposal only to recommend a method for an orderly transition of authority with respect to economic affairs. Palestinians should replace Israeli military officers at the helm of these agencies, but the existing bureaucracies and procedures should be left intact in order to provide the Palestinians with an organized point of departure. Subsequently, they obviously will develop their institutions as they see fit.[2]

Present governmental institutions for the Occupied Territories have evolved over the past 25 years by building on the institutions in existence just before the Israeli occupation. During the occupation, this structure was continually remolded by military orders. As of September 1992, the Civil Administration comprised three departments and various bureaus within departments dealing with the economy. (See Table 4.1 for a list of these departments and bureaus.)

The Civil Administration has field offices in Gaza, Hebron, Bethlehem, Ramallah, Tulkarm, Jenin, and representatives on the Jordan river bridges.

Most observers agree that, at least through early 1991, the rules and bureaucracy of the Civil Administration inhibited the economic development of the West Bank and Gaza. This is the case despite the relatively high rates of growth in gross domestic product and per capita income since 1967. It is true that in earlier years, the Israel Agricultural Extension Service helped introduce technological developments in agriculture. However, it is widely agreed that various bureaus in the Civil Administration often

---

2. When Israel assumed control from the British in 1948, its institutions were fused from those of the British Mandatory Administration and those of the pre-state Jewish national institutions.

undercut the interests of local firms and residents, if that served the policies of the Civil Administration. In particular, the Civil Administration foiled the development of modern manufacturing and needed financial institutions. Thus the failure of departments to render better services to the local economy may have been a function of Israeli policy rather than a manifestation of inherent organizational deficiencies in the Civil Administration.

There is no question that the bureaucratic structure of the Civil Administration will need to be changed to create an economic machinery more conducive to economic development. To take just one example, it is unclear why water resources are in a separate department (Department B) from agriculture and the major economic functions (Department C). The major question though is the timing of this transition process relative to the interim period. Is it advisable to proceed immediately with building a shadow set of alternative institutions, not necessarily congruent with existing ones, so that a new structure will be in place as soon as the transfer of authority takes place?

Our answer to this key question is no. We recommend instead that the present government machinery continue to function during the process leading to the inauguration of the interim authority, that it form the basis for the administrative structure during the period of interim self-government, and that the administrative structure should be adapted during and after the interim period. Underlying this approach are three considerations.

First, after decades of living under difficult circumstances, existing expertise among the Palestinians in the West Bank and Gaza needs to be enhanced to face the challenge of building economic institutions. The current situation is an understandable outcome of the low level of economic development during the occupation. Nurturing new institutions can better be accomplished once the new authority takes over, learns from experience the strengths and weaknesses of the current structures, and exercises its freedom to draw on domestic and foreign expertise, including that of Palestinians living in the diaspora.

Second, it is neither surprising nor detrimental to note that Palestinian society is currently characterized by deep fissures. Coming out of a period of military occupation, it is understandable that mechanisms will need to be developed to channel the natural differences in views that exist among the Palestinian people. If the process of recruiting new personnel for new institutions is conducted in the pre-interim stage, recruitment may be more influenced by factional loyalties than professional criteria. Our hope is that self-government will lessen factionalism.

Third, creating added uncertainty about the future of current government institutions and their personnel is likely to affect adversely the performance of these institutions. Without a commitment to start from the current structure, a very real danger exists that the public sector infrastructure will be severely damaged even before the start of the interim period. The interim self-governing authority will in any case be facing a daunting task of economic management, and it would be a mistake to add unnecessarily to that task by also requiring it to rebuild the structure of economic management from the ground up.

Further Recommendations Concerning Governmental Institutions

Taking over existing institutions is only the first step. We next have to consider the evolution of the self-governing authority from the point of view of building new economic institutions.

In planning for the administration of essential economic functions during the transition period, it is useful to start by making an inventory and analyzing the institutional resources that are available and required. The inventory should consider three types of institutions: (a) those currently engaged in the administration of essential functions; (b) those that will be needed to carry out new functions that will emerge as the transition proceeds; and (c) those, including NGOs (non-governmental organizations), which can support essential public activities and will continue to function in the future, perhaps in a somewhat changed form.

The first category, organizations performing essential functions, is likely to be part of the structure of the Israel Defense Forces Civil Administration. In analyzing these institutions, it is necessary first to consider in detail the functions and operations of these units in order to evaluate their compatibility with the functions of the expected self-governing authority (e.g., the analysis should consider the extent to which the "charter" of the units could be simply transferred to a successor organization). The analysis should also assess the degree to which the mandate of these organizations (their operational procedures as well as their assigned purposes) will have to change as the interim-period approaches. Secondly, the long term viability of the existing units can be appraised by evaluating the professional/technical qualifications of existing staff, especially of those who are likely to remain in office during the transition; and by planning training programs for technical and managerial staff.

The second category, organizations needed for essential functions that are not currently being performed, presents a more difficult challenge since the needs here will be determined by the political arrangements that govern the interim period. It is obvious that administrative functions that have not been needed under an occupation (such as trade policies) are likely to become very important to a self-governing Palestinian entity. Some of these functions may now be carried out by local municipal units, and by NGOs, which may continue to have a special interest and role in the provision of these services. While most of the analysis in this category will have to rest on uncertain assumptions about the future, it will nonetheless be necessary to think ahead about the needs in these categories, perhaps by considering needs based on different sets of assumptions.

The third category involves still greater uncertainty. This category includes functions that represent some prerogatives of sovereignty, such as participation in regional activities and ad hoc negotiations with parallel administrative units in Israel, Jordan, Egypt, and other countries. The identification of these functions cannot take place until the powers bestowed upon the self-governing authority in the transition process have become clear. In this category too, it will probably be useful to review the potential of organizations currently in existence even before the future political framework is fully clear.

No one should imagine that the ultimate structural decisions about organizing for the administration of economic functions will rest solely on rational principles of traditional public administration. Interest groups will surely play an active role in attempting to influence organizational decisions and in demanding specific services. No doubt Jordan and Israel will also attempt to exert influence. No modern society, whether a dictatorship or a democracy, is free of interest group politics; indeed, such politics are more prevalent in democratic than in totalitarian societies, and are an inherent part of the democratic process. As will be noted below, this fact should not be ignored with regard to the Palestinian entity.

Consistent with the major recommendation of this group, that the most efficient mechanism for transferring authority over governmental institutions is to start with existing institutions, we suggest the rapid but not precipitate replacement of Israelis in technical positions by Palestinians. It would not be useful to start wide-scale recruitment for new jobs during this period, before the needs of the interim self-governing authority have become clear.

Both before and after the interim self-governing authority assumes control, study teams comprised of local and expatriate experts should be commissioned to investigate all economic sectors and related institutions. This process has already begun, in part through this report, and in work requested from the World Bank in the context of the multilateral peace talks. More in-depth studies of the detailed needs of the interim self-governing authority should be undertaken as the beginning of the period of interim self-government comes closer and its political dimensions more clear.

To build the local economy and to enable the self-governing authority to manage it effectively, we recommend that:

• Within the framework of the negotiated agreement, the interim self-governing authority should be accorded effective legislative power regarding domestic economic matters. This should include not only the power to issue new laws and regulations, but also the authority—within the agreement—to amend and to abrogate laws inherited from previous authorities (Ottoman, British, Jordanian, and Israeli);

• It is both important for the Palestinian economy and of potential benefit to its neighboring countries that the interim self-governing authority be able to draw on the human and financial resources of other governments and international agencies. In some cases, the existing regulations of international agencies will be consistent with membership of the self-governing authority, and it should be permitted to join. Methods will need to be devised to enable the self-governing authority to be associated with international agencies such as the World Bank and the IMF which could contribute to the development of the West Bank and Gaza, but which require statehood as a prerequisite for membership. Trust funds provided by donor countries to be administered for the benefit of the West Bank and Gaza present one possible avenue through which such agencies could operate;

• Security measures should not be used in a punitive manner which hinders the development of the economy. Palestinian and Israeli authorities should find mutually acceptable means to handle common security concerns with minimal adverse consequences for their economies;

• The interim self-governing authority should receive from the Israeli occupation authorities all public and government-held records and data relevant to the management of the economy.

Palestinian Non-Governmental Institutions

There are several other sets of Palestinian institutions which have a strong bearing on the economy, though they are not part of the government structure. The most important of these institutions include: the higher education system, chambers of commerce, cooperative societies, credit institutions, and development centers.

One of the striking features of the institution-building process during the past twenty-five years is the large number of NGOs that has been established, and their impact on Palestinian economic activity. In response to the economic distortions resulting from occupation, local Palestinian as well as foreign NGOs have developed programs in many fields, including economic development, education, health, and social services. The combination of the strong preferences of the donor agencies and the absence of a Palestinian central authority has resulted in an apparent duplication of institutions and services. This has further distorted economic activity in the Territories. While the diversity of voluntary organizations that exists in any democratic society inevitably results in some degree of waste, the need to harmonize the priorities of the Palestinian leadership and those of external funding agencies poses a particular challenge for the interim self-governing authority.

Higher Education System

The Higher Council of Education is one of the few organizations in the West Bank and Gaza that aims to coordinate activities and resources for an entire sector. Nevertheless, the effectiveness of the system has been questioned on many occasions. It will be useful now to begin to analyze the structure of the present system and its objectives, and to propose measures of reform and reorganization to achieve these goals.

Cooperative Societies

By operating as businesses instead of non-profit organizations, cooperative societies—which are active in sectors such as agriculture—could play a more important role in the Palestinian economy. Doing so would free them of their present dependence on grants and force them to operate effectively.

Chambers of Commerce

In most countries, chambers of commerce play an important role in representing and promoting the interests of trade and industry. They operate not only as pressure groups with respect to government, but also as coordinating and implementing agencies for non-governmental functions such as establishing contacts with foreign counterparts, export-promotion and, in some cases, the setting of standards. In the time leading up to the interim period, the chambers of commerce in the West Bank and Gaza could play a facilitating role with regard to licensing, taxation, contacts with financial institutions, and the promotion of international trade. At the same time, it would be useful for the leaders of chambers of commerce to receive training in areas in which they will need expertise, such as management. This training could be provided either through courses and technical assistance in the West Bank and Gaza, or by courses and visiting programs abroad, not only at educational institutions, but also in the corporate sector. It would be important, as the interim period approaches, to reduce the factionalism of the chambers of commerce and to help them become more effective non-political promoters of the general interests of industry and trade.

Local Credit Institutions

The closure of local banks for the last twenty-five years has prompted those promoting economic development in the Occupied Territories to set up local credit institutions in an attempt to fill the gap. Aside from the commercial banks, there are four such institutions at the present, all of which are registered as non-profit companies and thriving on grants received from foreign donors, principally the European Community. The combined volume of loan funds available to all such non-bank local credit institutions amounts to roughly $3 million per year. It is quite clear, however, that because of their extremely limited financial resources, local non-bank credit institutions respond to only a small fraction of the applications received and thus create expectations which they cannot fulfill.

Consistent with the thrust of the report of the working group on the financial sector, any scheme of institutional development in the Palestinian entity must strengthen financial intermediation in the Occupied Territories. This will certainly involve the creation of new financial institutions and an expansion of total lending capacity. Existing non-bank credit institutions should be consolidated with other financial organizations and perhaps with each other during this process.

Development Centers

A great number of centers engage in data collection, economic research, and human resource development in the West Bank and Gaza. Development centers may provide the most serious example of extreme proliferation and factional affiliation among development institutions in the territories, and there is no question that the overlap among the activities of the centers is excessive.

The interim self-governing authority should evaluate the situation so as to reduce duplication without inhibiting the democratic diversity in which research flourishes. If the self-governing authority were successful in reducing the factional ties of these centers and in remolding them in accordance with both democracy and national needs, it could use similar methods to reduce excessively overlapping efforts in other areas.

We should however emphasize that some overlap and proliferation among private voluntary organizations is inevitable in any democratic society and that it is more a sign of the vigor of the society than of weakness. Thus, governments should intervene to try to reshape the structure of NGO systems only in extreme cases.

Foreign and United Nations Organizations
The West Bank and Gaza have witnessed an enormous surge of activity on the part of international agencies and foreign-based, non-political organizations during the past two decades. The bulk of these NGOs are European, but some are American, Australian, Canadian, and Japanese. The areas targeted by foreign NGOs touch on nearly every aspect of life in Palestinian society: economic development, education, health, rural development, and social services. In addition, several UN-affiliated organizations operate in the Occupied Territories. A partial list includes UNRWA, UNDP, UNCIAD, ESCWA, UNIDO, FAO, UNESCO, ILO, and WHO.

We have to recognize the role of UNRWA as a major provider of such basic services as primary health care, elementary and secondary education, manpower development and social welfare for around one-third of the population in the Occupied

Territories. UNRWA's annual budget amounted in 1992 to roughly $120 million; and it employs roughly 8,000 people in the West Bank and Gaza. UNRWA is expected to perform the same functions during the interim period. UNRWA should draw on technical assistance to improve and expand its services. The new entity can draw on UNRWA's expertise in areas like primary health care and manpower development.

The contribution of foreign NGOs in the area of economic development is debatable. The effectiveness of the UN institutions is also difficult to judge. Observers, particularly residents of the Occupied Territories, see a great need for better coordination, clearer priorities, and less politicization among them in order to reduce duplication and to use limited and much needed resources to better effect.

Chapter 7 of this report suggests that the interim self-governing authority should set up a unified agency to deal with foreign aid. This agency would take the lead in coordinating and guiding the activities of the existing external aid agencies as well as those of new agencies that will become active once the interim period begins.

An Institutional Structure for PISGA

Following the opening phase of the interim period—when existing institutions will be kept in place—new institutions will have to be created to manage the economy. Hence, we sketch below the outlines of a "young" economic structure. Two points should help clarify the basis for this structure. First, the set of indicated governmental responsibilities reflects the understandings and recommendations reached by this and the five other working groups organized for this project. Obviously, it is the responsibilities or functions that we previously suggested for the interim self-governing authority that result in our recommendations for its institutional structure. For example, our group agreed that there should be a single foreign aid agency within the self-governing authority, both to plan the aid needs of the West Bank and Gaza and to coordinate negotiations and interactions with donor organizations. Another example is the agreement of this group that if the Palestinians are to control their own economy, they must also control the geographical placement of infrastructure and enterprises. Second, the structure outlined below provides a conception of the institutions that would be needed for the guidance of the Palestinian economy and its integration with Israel and Jordan by the end of the interim period. The evolution of this structure from the existing institutions (basically out of Department C of the Civil Administration) is not addressed in this chapter and obviously requires further consideration.

Our sketch of a government structure is divided into six parts. With respect to each, we first indicate the responsibilities of the department and then list its component bureaus. It is important to note that, in the end, it will be up to the self-governing authority to design its own institutional structure. What follows is intended for the use of those designing the evolving structure.

Department of Finance

This central economic department would be responsible for presenting and managing the annual budget. It would thus need to set and coordinate the priorities for spending in the public sector, and to provide the revenue to finance the outlays of the interim authority. While the annual budget would be the focus of the department's activities, the preparation of a multi-year budget would enhance budget planning and discipline. This budget could be revised each year on the basis of changing economic conditions.

The department would develop an internal revenue service and the Palestinian social protection system. The Department of Finance would also begin to consider macro-economic fiscal policy. For this purpose it might want to set up a bureau of policy and planning.

In light of the likely importance of foreign aid to the Palestinian economy in its early years, we recommend that the management of foreign aid be assigned to a special agency in the Department of Finance. The Foreign Aid Agency would manage all foreign aid operations, negotiate with donors and coordinate with the budget planning bureau.

The major bureaus of the Finance Department would include:

- Expenditure planning and control
- Internal revenue service
- Foreign aid
- Social protection
- Policy and planning.

Department of Industry, Trade, and Tourism

Consistent with the intention of developing a market-oriented free enterprise economy, this department would be responsible for the promotion of business activity, including exports, as well as its regulation. It would be responsible for licensing commercial, industrial, tourist, and other types of firms and would also regulate their activities in accordance with legislation and regulations.

This department would be responsible for the promotion and regulation of international trade and in that context would administer trade regulations. These should include the promotion of exports from the West Bank and Gaza, an area in which international technical expertise can be mobilized. The department might also eventually collect customs fees and duties. Such departments often become strong forces for protection, and it would be important in establishing regulations to try to ensure that they do not unnecessarily impede international trade.

The department would also supervise joint ventures and other economic activities with foreign countries. It would establish and regulate product standards. The department might encourage the development of industrial and free trade zones and coordinate its work with chambers of commerce. Finally, it would control and regulate the use of land and the environment.

Its bureaus would include:

- Corporate promotion and licensing
- Product standards
- Export promotion
- Imports
- Environmental protection
- Land management (zoning, special zones, etc.)

Department of Economic Development

This department would direct economic development policy and the provision of infrastructure for a market-oriented, private enterprise-dominated Palestinian economy. It would be necessary for this department to coordinate closely with the other economic departments, the Department of Finance and the Department of Industry, Trade and Tourism (DITT), so that development and infrastructure planning would be consistent with the promotion of the private sector, which will be the main focus of the DITT, and with the availability of financing, which will be the responsibility of the Department of Finance.[3]

---

3. Sectoral bureaus should take into serious consideration the prospect of having a seaport in Gaza as well as Palestinian air transport and railway facilities.

Its bureaus would include:

- Economic development planning
- Sectoral bureaus:
  Transportation
  Communications
  Public Works
  Energy
  Housing
  Agriculture
  Tourism
  Manufacturing
  Water

Department of Human Resources

This department would manage a wide variety of essential activities pertaining to the Palestinian labor force both inside and outside the self-governed area; and the management of returning refugees, as agreed to in the anticipated, politically-negotiated agreement on an interim self-governing authority.

Its bureaus would include:

- Education
- Training
- Absorption and registration
- Labor standards

Independent Agencies

Several agencies should be free-standing and report directly to the head of the interim self-governing authority.

These agencies include:

- Central Bureau of Statistics
- Civil Service Administration.

Financial and Monetary Authority

In Chapter 6 of this report, we describe the functions of a Palestinian Interim Financial and Monetary Authority (PIMFA), which we envisage as having a separate and independent identity from the rest of the self-governing authority.

The major task of this authority would be to develop and regulate a set of financial institutions and intermediaries, so as to improve the efficiency of the payments mechanism and to channel savings from households to firms requiring capital, thereby helping to develop the economy. The authority should therefore: charter, supervise, and regulate new banks in the West Bank and Gaza (in coordination with the authorities in Jordan and Israel); supervise and regulate the existing commercial Palestinian banks; charter and supervise non-bank financial intermediaries; and collect and publish data on the financial system.

To address the above functions, we recommend that the PIMFA have several bureaus:

- Banking
- Non-bank financial institutions
- External economic relations
- Research, statistics, and economic policy.

Alternative Institutional Arrangements

We should emphasize that the departmental structure proposed in this section provides one possible option, but that others may be equally efficient. Two strategic choices should be noted. First, we have located the Foreign Aid Agency in the Department of Finance. This suggestion is based on two considerations: foreign financing will provide a large share of the revenues available to the self-governing authority in the early stages, and the Department of Finance should therefore be involved in the coordination of this financing; and the Department of Finance's control over aggregate spending will be enhanced if it is directly involved in discussions of projects to be financed by foreign assistance. There are also strong external grounds for putting this agency in the Department of Economic Development, for there is no question that foreign financing and interactions with the international agencies will play a key role in development planning. But we have chosen the former arrangement, that in the Department of Finance.

Second, there is also a strong case for an alternative structure in which there is no Department of Economic Development and its functions are split between the Departments of Finance and DITT. In this arrangement, the infrastructure and development functions would be placed in the Department of Finance. This would ensure that foreign aid and development planning responsibilities are located within the same department, which would be a major advantage. The sectoral responsibilities of the former Department of Economic Development would be placed in the reconstituted DITT, which would then be renamed the Department of Industry and Trade.

Because responsibilities always overlap, there is no unique most efficient administrative structure. International experience does suggest that the proliferation of departments under separate political heads reduces the effectiveness of economic management. One guiding principle could be that when in doubt, potential departments should be consolidated rather than separated.

Coordination Between Palestinian and Neighboring Economies

While it is not the task of this project to consider either the interim or the ultimate political status of the Occupied Territories, we have had to make assumptions about the economic power of the Palestinian entity as well as about its economic relationships with Israel and Jordan. We have assumed that within the agreed political framework, the Palestinian entity will have both economic sovereignty and relatively open borders with Israel and Jordan. Indeed, a peace with closed borders between the Palestinian entity and its two neighbors is unlikely to attract international financial support

Certainly for the transition period, and, we believe, for the longer term as well, the three parties should agree upon a mechanism to deal with matters of mutual interest on a continuing basis—perhaps in the form of a "high liaison coordinating council." This council should form working groups in areas in which the economic policies of one of the parties would have a substantial impact on that of the other two.

The three parties are so close to each other geographically, and their economies are so likely to become intertwined, that coordination in a variety of areas is called for. The need for such coordination is self-evident. Value added taxes that are not harmonized would have adverse consequences for legitimate cross-border trade as would differences in trade regulations with respect to third parties. Non-uniform product standards would undermine the standards of the entity with the most demanding standard. The same is true regarding standards for professionals. While the present structure of the PIMFA takes the need for coordination of certain financial policies into account by including both Bank of Jordan and Central Bank of Israel representatives, at a later stage it would likely be necessary also to coordinate aspects of monetary and exchange rate policy. A regional development bank obviously requires the membership of all three parties.

In general, the three parties need to conclude comprehensive trade, commercial, and banking treaties. They should seek to undertake projects of common interest where the economies of scale will yield gains for all three parties. The parties need to coordinate policies and their implementation on an on-going basis. Towards this end, we propose, in preparation for the transition, the formation of the high liaison economic coordinating council.

5   Fiscal Management

Thomas C. Schelling, *Chair;* Atef Alawnah,
Daniel Gottlieb, Amin Haddad, Khalil Hammad,
Ephraim Kleiman, Efraim Sadka

The character of the fiscal arrangements that will need to be made, and the fiscal problems that will need to be solved in the West Bank and Gaza and among the three economies, pivot on a fundamental issue. The issue is whether the evolution of the transition period is to be toward granting maximum (or at least substantial) economic separation for the Palestinian entity, or is instead to be directed toward preserving and enhancing the movement of goods and services, labor, consumers, and capital among Israel and the two components of the Palestinian entity, and perhaps, equally, Jordan.

This issue pervades the entire report, and the general conclusion has been reached that freedom of trade and factor movements is most likely to promote the well-being of all three groups. Accordingly we devote considerable attention in this chapter to both fiscal arrangements and parameters in the West Bank and Gaza, and to the potential difficulties that would be created by non-uniform systems and rates of taxation in the different entities.

We start by reviewing information about the current state of fiscal affairs in the Occupied Territories. We then go on to discuss tax issues, social security, and infrastructure needs. We identify the tax and social security issues, and where appropriate make recommendations about the types of systems that are likely to work well.

We do not have sufficient information to present a detailed description of the likely future revenue needs and resources of the self-governing authority. We do have enough information to suggest that the tax system now in place is capable of generating an amount of revenue that is not out of line with the average for a country with an income level similar to that of the West Bank and Gaza.

Some Fiscal Background

GDP and GNP figures for the West Bank, Gaza, and for the combined Territories are presented in Table 2-1 in Chapter 2. The Occupied Territories' per capita income of $1800 puts them in the World Bank's middle income category. Tax revenues in such countries average around 18-22 percent of GDP, with the ratio for the Middle East being a little above average. Government revenue from all sources averages 24 percent of GDP, and expenditures 27.5 percent of GDP for such countries—with a wide range around each average.[1]

In Table 5.1 we present estimates of the taxes paid by residents of the West Bank and Gaza in 1991. The data under items B and C are less accurate than those under A; in particular, the VAT paid on imports from Israel is difficult to estimate, since it is based on an estimate of the import surplus of the Territories from Israel. The amounts shown here should be augmented by $14 million of income taxes on workers from the Territories,

1. Data are from *World Development Report*, 1988, Chapters 2 and 4. The difference between GNP and GDP is much smaller for most countries than for the West Bank and Gaza, and it is reasonable to think of these as ratios to GNP as well as GDP. These data are from the mid-1980s, but there has been little trend in spending or revenues since then.

Table 5.1
Estimates of the Revenues Originating in the West Bank and Gaza, 1991[a] ($ million[b])

A. Revenues Collected by the Civil Administration		
West Bank		147.4
Income tax	44.4	
VAT	46.5	
Excise duty	31.3	
Gaza		38.1
Income tax	23.5	
Vehicle taxes	13.0	
B. Taxes on Imports		89.1
On direct imports via Israel	40.3	
On fuel	44.8	
C. VAT on Imports from Israel	109.7	
Total:		**384.3**

As a share of GNP: 13.3 %
As a share of GDP: 18.0 %

a. Based on tax collection data for the West Bank and Gaza, augmented in items B and C by information published by Zeev Schiff in *Haaretz*.
b. Original data in shekels, translated at the average exchange rate for 1991.

deducted at source in Israel. Taxes paid by Palestinians as a share of GDP are thus not dissimilar to the average for middle income countries. However, the large gap between GNP and GDP means that taxes are low as a share of GNP.

The Civil Administration's budgeted spending for 1991 is presented in Table 5.2.[2] Total spending exceeds revenues collected in the Territories, but falls short of the total taxes paid by Palestinian residents of the West Bank and Gaza. Development expenditures are very small as a share of GDP.

Municipal budgets in 1991 amounted to a total of nearly $50 million, about 2.5 percent of GDP. The municipalities' main source of income is sales of electricity and water; in addition they receive small amounts of revenue from fees, and from the Civil Administration. Municipal capital spending is very low.

2. Of course, the Civil Administration budget does not include Israeli defense spending in the Territories.

Table 5.2
Civil Administration Budget, Uses, 1991 ($ million[a])

West Bank		
Current expenditure		174.9
Health	26.4	
Education	59.0	
Development expenditure		30.5
Gaza		
Current expenditure		81.7
Health	21.6	
Education	21.1	
Development expenditure		12.2
Development reserve[b]	15.9	
Total:		**315.2**

As a share of GNP: 11.0 %
As a share of GDP: 14.9 %

a. Underlying data are specified in shekels, at "1992 budget prices." We have translated these into dollars at the average exchange rate for 1992.
b. The nature of this reserve is not known to us.

The fiscal picture is thus one in which the fiscal apparatus is already collecting sizable revenues from the Palestinians in the West Bank and Gaza, and in which both an income tax and a VAT are already in place. The self-governing authority will thus have access to a functioning fiscal system from the beginning. No doubt, there will at some point be a need to reform the tax system and make it more coherent, but that does not appear to be a crucial immediate need. The municipalities function, albeit with small budgets, but not budgets that are out of the normal range for municipalities.[3]

Tax Issues

The assumption that the currently more or less free movement of goods and services and, to a somewhat lesser extent, also of

3. This statement is based on data in Figure 7.1, p. 155 of the *World Development Report*, 1988.

labor between the Territories and Israel will be maintained in the interim period, raises important tax issues, not least that of tax coordination. Such issues have of course arisen forcefully with the move to a single market in Europe.

Tax Coordination and Revenue

The two principal kinds of tax issues that need to be considered can be briefly characterized as tax coordination and revenue recovery. Each can be simply illustrated. First, tax coordination. Taxes on such standardized brand-name commodities as gasoline and cigarettes can lead to visible and easily measurable price differences; excise tax differences on these commodities will almost certainly be reflected in their retail prices. Significant tax differences cannot exist in an economic region as small as Israel and the Palestinian entity without diverting customers in large numbers from the higher to the lower tax region. Not only is such diversion wasteful of consumer time and gasoline, but it can lead to "tax competition" between the two tax regions, as has been observed frequently in the United States. There are limits to the departures from tax uniformity between the two regions that can exist without causing mischief, the magnitude of which will depend on the nature of the commodity and its transportability. Thus, some coordination of tax rates is required.

Revenue recovery is illustrated by the value added tax (VAT) and by import duties. Even if there is adequate coordination of VATs between the two regions to eliminate artificial price discrepancies, Palestinians will be paying Israeli VAT on goods produced in Israel while Israelis will be paying Palestinian VAT on goods produced in the Palestinian entity. If trade in these taxed items were perfectly balanced, the Israeli and Palestinian tax authorities would each be collecting exactly the revenues paid by their own citizens. There is currently a sizable discrepancy between VAT-taxed items purchased by Palestinians in Israel and VAT-taxed purchases by Israelis in the West Bank and Gaza. As a result, Palestinian consumers are paying more VAT to Israeli fiscal authorities than vice versa. If the object of the VAT is to tax consumption, then Israel is taxing Palestinian consumption (and thus consumers) more than the West Bank and Gaza are taxing Israeli consumption (and thus consumers).

Similarly, when Palestinians purchase goods imported through Israel from the rest of the world, the import duties collected by the Israeli authorities are ultimately paid for by the Palestinian final purchaser. Both the VAT and customs duties generate net revenues for Israel which are paid by Palestinians; therefore, a negotiated formula for recovering these revenues is clearly called for. Those purchase taxes that are levied at the factory gate rather than at the retail level raise the same issue of revenue recovery.

The revenue recovery issue is a crucial one. As Table 5.1 shows, almost one half the taxes paid by Palestinians in the West Bank and Gaza accrue to the Israeli tax authorities as either import duties or VAT. Thus the formula that specifies the basis on which revenues will be remitted to the self-governing authority will be a key determinant of its total revenues and ability to spend.

Coordination of customs duties will also be required. Even a small differential between the tariffs of Israel and the self-governing authority could reroute imports through the lower tariff area, thus avoiding the customs regime of the other. This problem is avoided in a customs union, the members of which specify a common external tariff, and agree on a basis for sharing the tariff revenues. The problem is far more difficult in a free trade area, whose members permit free trade with each other while permitting differences in tariffs against non-members. Rules of origin are used in free trade areas to try to prevent evasion of the higher customs duties, but these systems are imperfect and bureaucratically expensive. It would certainly be easier for Israel and the West Bank and Gaza to maintain free trade if they continued, as now, with a common external tariff.

Israel would make a customs union more attractive for the Palestinians if it proposed an equitable basis for sharing customs revenues. Maintenance of a customs union would also be much more likely if Israel sharply speeded up its proposed tariff reforms against non-EC, non-US goods. Agreement between the Palestinian self-governing authority and Israel on very low or zero tariffs against goods from Jordan and the rest of the Arab world would further enhance the likelihood of maintenance of a customs union. If trade opens up with Jordan, as we propose, the customs union should include Jordan.

Tax Levels

The VAT was discussed above with reference to the need for similar, if not uniform, rates. But a question immediately arises: what if the two authorities estimates their needs for revenue in such fashion that (as appears likely) Israel settles on a VAT of, say 17%, while the Palestinian entity, with lesser fiscal needs (e.g. no large defense establishment to maintain), prefers a VAT of, say, 7%. The same question could arise between Jordan and the Palestinian entity. A discrepancy of 10% may turn out to be extremely troublesome, causing trade diversion and tax avoidance. Yet Israel may find the revenue from a 17% tax essential while the Palestinian entity may consider a rate much above 7% intolerable.

A compromise figure like 11% may prove thoroughly unsatisfactory to both sides. It would be above the Palestinian preferred level by more than half, while it would reduce Israeli VAT revenues by more than a third from the preferred level. In theory a uniform Israeli tariff of 10% against Palestinian goods would "equalize" the disparate VATs of 7% and 17%. But it would eliminate many of the virtues of freer trade, would exclude services, and would be difficult to apply ad valorem.

The difference in total revenue would, of course, be much greater for Israel than for the Palestinian entity, simply because total value added in Israel is so much greater. Moreover, with a lower Palestinian VAT, Israel would be the one to lose business through trade diversion. Conceivably some kind of compensation from Israel could offset the hardship of a higher VAT paid by Palestinians. But the problem for the Palestinians would not be fiscal cash flow—they would already be collecting double their desired VAT. Perhaps Israeli compensation could be used to lower taxes elsewhere, although lower excise taxes cause the same problem to reappear. We see no easy solution. Israel may have to acknowledge a Palestinian claim to a somewhat lower VAT with the attendant diversion of trade to the Territories.

Income Taxation

The corporate income tax poses a potential problem if tax rates are to differ between the self-governing authority and Israel, or the former and Jordan. There is always the risk of the Palestinian entity providing a tax shelter for Israeli (or Jordanian) firms and vice versa. This issue can be resolved in two ways. First, uniform corporate income tax rates can be instituted. Second, agreements can be negotiated under which the income of Israeli-owned (Jordanian owned) corporations registered in the Territories is deemed to be produced in Israel (Jordan) and is subject to tax under the Israeli (Jordanian) rates; alternatively, Israel (Jordan) can tax the income of Israeli (Jordanian) firms operating in the Palestinian entity and allow a foreign tax credit against taxes paid in the Territories.

Similarly, with personal income taxes, an agreement will be required to prevent double taxation and to provide mutual disclosure of cross-residencies. There is no obvious unique principle to settle the jurisdictional issues of personal income taxation; as between most countries, agreements on this issue would have to be negotiated.

A special problem arises with regard to social security payments. As discussed in Chapter 3, social security taxes are imposed on wages earned in Israel by Palestinian work-permit holders who do not qualify for most of Israel's national insurance benefits. To avoid making Palestinian workers cheaper than Israeli ones, it seems likely that the taxes on both the worker and the employer will be maintained. It can be argued that these funds should not be retained for Israeli social security; however, there is currently no Palestinian social security system to which the funds could be directed, nor is it likely that any Palestinian social security system would be able to offer benefits to these Palestinian workers in Israel at the level of Israeli benefits, for some time to come. There needs to be a negotiated understanding concerning the allocation of these funds. The issue of social security taxes on Palestinian workers in Israel is discussed further in Chapter 3.

None of these issues—what the common level of VAT ought to be, what the revenue recovery formula or formulae ought to be, how to agree on specific import duties, etc.—can be dealt with in detail by this group. This is therefore an illustrative survey of the kinds of issues that must be addressed. It is not exhaustive, and we have suggested only the kinds of solutions that may be appealing. Again, the major categories are tax rate coordination and revenue recovery. As the need for uniform or similar tax rates becomes less, the more restrictive trade between the two regions could become. Correspondingly, with diminished economic integration of the two big regions, revenue recovery becomes less significant.

One aspect of taxation, which is not strictly fiscal, has been neglected here. That is that taxes serve a number of policy ends besides the provision of revenue. (In the United States, for example, taxes are used or proposed to discourage smoking, to reduce the use of fossil fuels, and to shape the distribution of income after taxes.) We considered this topic to be outside our terms of reference.

Social Security

Two kinds of issues arise with reference to social security for the residents of the new Palestinian self-governing authority. The lesser concern, already touched on under taxation, is how to reconcile what are bound to be the very disparate social security systems of Israel and the self-governing authority. That issue is better treated under the heading of taxation than social security. The main question, then, is what kind of social security system should be contemplated during the transition and what should be its ultimate goal.

At the outset it has to be emphasized that income per capita in the Palestinian entity will, for many years, perhaps even decades, be substantially lower than that of neighboring Israel. In searching for a social security system which the Palestinians will be able to afford, we could look to Jordan as a possible example. That system displays several characteristics worth noticing. One is that pension funds for public employees, both civilian and military, constitute a full-blown system which is separate from the system for laborers in the private sector. The second is that, in the private sector, the social security system began with modest coverage and progressively extended its coverage, as was the case in many countries including the United

States. A third characteristic is that certain kinds of employment and employees are more readily extended coverage than others; thus, for example, regular workers in large plants are more easily integrated into the system than domestic servants, the self-employed, sailors, fishermen, and farmers. Furthermore, the Jordanian system is imbedded in a Muslim tradition that provides charitable contributions outside the official social security system.

The key question is whether to include health care as an integral part of the social security system. At least two characteristics separate health care in the West Bank and Gaza from the other elements commonly included in the umbrella of social security such as retirement, employment, welfare, child care, and disability. One is that in most countries, including Israel and in the West Bank and Gaza, there has developed a strong tradition that medical care is a public responsibility. A second is that health care has proved immensely popular as a target of foreign aid. According to the report of the foreign aid group (Chapter 7), 42% of all foreign aid to the West Bank and Gaza in 1992 went to comprehensive health services, disease prevention and control, and environmental health. A large part of that went to public health infrastructure; but several tens of millions of foreign aid went into hospitals, clinics, and medical services.[4] We believe that the politics and public relations of maximizing the appeal of Palestinian health care to public and private agencies abroad strongly implies keeping health care financially and institutionally separate from the other components of a social security system.

For the other components of social security, most of which involve financial assistance rather than assistance in kind, we

---

4. We do not have a breakdown, but it seems likely that these foreign aid contributions to health care among Palestinians includes both official foreign aid from governments and international institutions, and contributions from private voluntary organizations and foundations.

believe the new Palestinian entity should begin modestly, not ambitiously, should recognize that traditional reliance on family care should continue to be a significant form of social security, and might well study the experience of Jordan.

A major distinction with respect to retirement systems, but also unemployment compensation systems and disability compensation systems, is between those that closely link benefits to contributions, and those that are part of the general revenue system. This distinction corresponds closely to, but is not identical with, the distinction between "defined benefit" and "defined contribution" systems.

The argument for tying benefits to contributions is at least two-fold. One is that people may be much more willing to contribute through taxation to a retirement system if doing so provides a claim on benefits that are not indiscriminately available to everyone else. A second is that it disciplines a government in providing only what the economy can afford.

The balance of logic and experience suggests that a system with the following features makes the most sense: one that links benefits to contributions; one that limits initial coverage to workers in regular employment in establishments capable of being adequately monitored and administered; and one that can grow as the economy modernizes.

Economic Infrastructure Needs

A survey of infrastructure needs to identify projects and their levels of urgency and priority will be a high priority for the interim government; it can also help to measure the magnitude of the fiscal problem. Currently, we do not have reconciled figures on joint expenditures for public services and investments or current revenues corresponding to the taxes paid by Palestinians. Thus we do not have a numerical framework within which to fit infrastructure needs which would enable us to measure the adequacy or inadequacy of likely available resources. We believe the World Bank may have access to such data and may be able to begin work on the needed survey. Like health care, infrastructure is an area likely to be attractive to providers of foreign aid. For example, the World Bank is experienced in aiding infrastructure projects. Similarly, national governments and non-governmental organizations (NGOs) typically support tangible projects such as physical structures. Developers of a ten-year program for infrastructure need to consider carefully not only the levels of urgency and priority of particular projects, but also their marketability for governments and NGOs interested in financing them. We distinguish between urgencies and priorities. Roughly speaking, priority refers to the importance of including an item in the long range plan, while urgency refers to the timing of the completion of a project.

While we do not have an integrated framework for assessing infrastructure needs, we do have a number of estimates of orders of magnitude of expenditure on different projects. We present them, to fix these orders of magnitude in mind.

Currently about 80% of annual health expenditures in the Occupied Territories comes from external national and international organizations. It is worth noting that per capita annual health care expenditures in the Occupied Territories is about $100, compared with $500 in Israel. There is an estimate according to which a one-time initial capital investment of $450 million US dollars is an appropriate investment target in the near term.

Briefly, to give some order of magnitude, the estimated cost of a five year water development plan for the Occupied Territories is about $75 million, which would include rehabilitation of old municipal wells, drilling of new wells, installation of main water pipes, and rehabilitation of current and development of new required water distribution systems. Sanitation and treatment of waste water in the next few years could apparently absorb $60 or $70 million. Electricity and power may require investment of between $100 and $150 million. Transportation can apparently absorb a billion dollars or more. That would include a road network at over $600 million, a new public transportation system at $40 million, sea transportation including the Gaza port at $50 or $60 million, airport facilities and others.

None of these figures should be taken altogether seriously, since they are a collection of estimates from different sources. They are not based on estimated urgencies and priorities, and it is not clear how steeply the marginal value goes down as the lower priority projects are included. If one roughly adds the infrastructure needs under these several headings, recognizes that the list is incomplete, and supposes that most of what is needed takes at least several years to complete, an exceedingly rough order of magnitude might be a need for investment in infrastructure of $3 billion over ten years, or an average of $300 million in 1993 dollars per year. That kind of figure needs to be fitted into the fiscal framework and the prospects for foreign aid over the coming decade.

6 Financial and Monetary Arrangements in the Palestinian Transition

Lester C. Thurow, *Chair*; Ibrahim Affaneh,
Daniel Gottlieb, Khalil Hammad, Hisham Jabr,
Leonardo Leiderman, Zvi Sussman

The Current Situation

Current financial and monetary arrangements in the Occupied
Territories reflect the results of Israeli policy since 1967. Before
the 1967 War, the Jordanian dinar was the legal tender in the
West Bank, and the Egyptian pound was the legal tender in the
Gaza Strip. Now both the Israeli shekel and the dinar are legal
tender on the West Bank. While only the shekel is legal tender
in Gaza, the dinar is also widely used.

In May 1967 there were eight banks with a total of 31 branches operating in East Jerusalem and the West Bank, of which five
were in East Jerusalem. There were three banks with a total of
eight branches in Gaza.[1] After the 1967 War, these banks were
closed and Israeli banks were opened. Table 6.1 shows subse-
quent changes in the number of bank branches.

In October 1986, the Cairo-Amman Bank was reopened on
the West Bank, after a tacit agreement between the central
banks of Jordan and Israel. It has branches in Nablus, Jenin,
Tulkarm, Hebron, Bethlehem and two in Ramallah. The Bank of

---

1. Data on the total number of branches in 1967 are taken from Laurence Harris,
"Money and Finance with Undeveloped Banking in the Occupied Territories," in
George T. Abed, ed., *The Palestinian Economy*, (New York: Routledge, 1988).

Palestine was opened in Gaza in 1981; it now has branches in Gaza, Khan Yunis and Jabaliya. Negotiations involving the Israeli and Jordanian authorities have been proceeding for some time about the possibility of opening branches of the (commercial) Bank of Jordan on the West Bank, and there is now some expectation that three branches will open before the end of 1993.

In addition to the commercial banks, various other institutions provide financial services to the inhabitants of the Territories: moneychangers, commercial banks in Jordan and Israel, and some non-bank intermediaries in the West Bank and Gaza. The number of moneychangers increased rapidly following the closing of the Arab banks—from 42 in 1967 to 162 in 1986. Moneychangers are legally permitted to exchange shekels for dinars, but they also engage in activities such as buying and selling other currencies, arranging money transfers, accepting some deposits, and making loans to customers they know well. Naturally, information about the volume and range of these activities is scant. Data on transactions between Jordanian and Israeli banks, respectively, and residents of the Territories is also unavailable.

Money Holdings in the West Bank and Gaza

Estimates of the amount of money held in the West Bank and Gaza vary widely: estimates of the ratio of M1 (currency plus demand deposits) to GDP range from 40 percent to 75 percent. The unknown in these estimates is holdings of currency (dinars, shekels, and other currencies). The comparable ratio for Israel is 6 percent, for Egypt 22 percent, and for Jordan 57 percent.[2]

---

2. However, 57 percent is certainly too high as an estimate of holdings of M1 to GDP *in Jordan*, since that number is calculated as the ratio of total Jordanian dinar M1 to Jordanian GDP, and part of the stock of dinar M1 is held in the West Bank and Gaza.

Table 6.1
Bank Branches Operating in the West Bank and Gaza Strip[3]

	1967	1986	1992
West Bank			
In Arab Towns:			
Arab banks	19	1	7
Israeli banks		11	3
Total	19	12	10
In Israeli Settlements:		10	10
Gaza			
In Arab Towns			
Arab banks	4	1	3
Israeli banks		5	0
Total	4	6	3
In Israeli Settlements:		3	3

Whatever the precise number, there is no doubt that money holdings in the West Bank and Gaza are very high relative to GDP, by international standards. There is, further, no question that the bulk of M1 is held in the form of currency, and not bank deposits.

There are good reasons for these phenomena. Money holdings are high because economic life in the West Bank and Gaza is subject to many shocks, and money serves as a shock absorber. The absence of ready access to short-term credit increases the need to hold money. These money holdings take the form of currency rather than deposits because depositors are uncertain as to whether deposits are consistently secure and quickly accessible under military administration.

The existence of such large money holdings means that there is a considerable potential for the development of banking in the West Bank and Gaza. The saving rate is high on average,

---

3. Excluding East Jerusalem.

especially in Gaza,[4] and people have large stocks of liquid savings. If financial institutions develop, within a framework that reassures potential depositors of the safety of their deposits and that pays interest on deposits, large amounts of cash can be moved into the financial intermediary system, and bank-mediated lending can develop rapidly.

Thus the West Bank and Gaza already have one of the essential ingredients for the creation of an active and vigorous system of financial intermediation—savings.

Bank Regulation in the Occupied Territories

Israeli banks are permitted to open branches in the West Bank and Gaza, subject to the approval of the Bank of Israel. Their operations are supervised by the Bank of Israel and they are essentially treated on the same basis as bank branches in Israel. The one exception is that Arab residents of the Territories are permitted to open dinar accounts.

Regulatory arrangements for the Cairo-Amman Bank may provide some useful precedents for the transition period.[5] Only Jordanian citizens resident on the West Bank can open accounts and take loans—in either dinars or shekels—with the Bank. Israeli settlers cannot use Jordanian banks.

The Cairo-Amman Bank is supervised jointly by the Central Bank of Jordan and the Bank of Israel. All dinar transactions are supervised by the Central Bank of Jordan, while transactions in shekels and other currencies are supervised by the Bank of

---

4. The rate of saving fluctuates a great deal, reflecting the buffer stock role of saving, which is lower in hard times than in good times that are expected to be temporary. The average saving rate (out of disposable income) in Gaza over the period 1970-83 was above 25 percent, with the comparable figure for the West Bank being 15 percent. Both these rates are high by international standards. They declined after 1985.

5. Negotiations are presently underway with the Bank of Jordan, a commercial bank, to open branches in the West Bank.

Israel. The Bank is subject to capital requirements imposed by the Bank of Jordan, as well as to supplementary but thus far non-binding capital ratios imposed by the Israel Defense Force's Civilian Administration. The military government imposes reserve requirements for non-dinar accounts similar to those for Israeli banks. These too have been non-binding. Whereas Israeli banks frequently use the discount window of the Bank of Israel, this has not been necessary thus far for the Cairo-Amman Bank.

There is no formal deposit insurance in either Israel or Jordan, though it is considered likely that the Central Bank of Jordan would effectively back dinar deposits if necessary, and that the Bank of Israel would similarly back shekel deposits.

The Bank of Palestine in Gaza has grown only slowly. It is regulated by the military, along the same lines as banks on the West Bank, but with only shekel accounts. There are no foreign banks in the Occupied Territories. The stated policy of the Israeli government has been to encourage the entrance of foreign banks into Israel, provided they meet certain criteria of minimum size, stability, and broad foreign base, but at present no deposit-taking foreign banks of any size operate in either Israel or the Occupied Territories. Seven foreign banks, with a total of 42 branches, including the British Bank of the Middle East, the Arab Land Bank, and Grindley's operate in Jordan.

Capital Controls in Israel and Jordan

Israeli regulations encourage foreign capital investments in Israel, but there are severe restrictions on foreign transactions for Israelis, especially of individuals. Resident individuals are not allowed to invest directly abroad or to purchase real estate, money market securities and non-listed securities abroad. They can, however, acquire foreign stocks. While not permitted to hold foreign bank accounts, except while temporarily resident abroad, Israeli residents can hold several types of foreign currency accounts in Israeli banks. There are fewer controls on firms. They have more scope to invest abroad, they can issue stock on foreign stock exchanges, and they can hold 10 percent of export proceeds in foreign bank accounts. Israeli mutual funds can also hold limited amounts of foreign assets.

In brief, Israeli controls on a wide range of potential capital movements by individuals remain in place, and some aspects of firms' capital movements are controlled. The extent of these controls has been gradually reduced in the years since 1985, and continues to be reduced.

The Jordanian system is more open to the inward or outward movement of capital by individuals. This difference creates a potential problem for Israeli capital controls, since free trade in goods and capital between Israel and the West Bank and Gaza and, in due course, Jordan, would give Israelis access to a less controlled financial system, and thereby enable them to evade their country's capital controls (see below).

The Goals of Financial Sector Development in the Occupied Territories

Any financial system should provide four essential sets of services. A stable monetary framework, reflected in low and stable inflation and stable exchange rates, is needed, as well as an efficient payments system in both domestic and international trade. In addition, there should be a system of financial intermediation which encourages saving and productive investment, as well as the efficient allocation of investment. Finally, there should be efficient sharing of risk in the economy, for instance through the provision of insurance.

In the Occupied Territories, the first of these services is now simply a function of how well Israeli and Jordanian economic policies are working, and the last three are poorly done. The monetary framework in the Occupied Territories is a complex composite of the Israeli and Jordanian systems. The use of both the Israeli and Jordanian currencies has the benefit of simplifying transactions with these two economies, at the expense of complicating economic transactions within the Occupied Territories. Monetary instability in Israel, now greatly reduced, and some recent exchange rate instability in Jordan, automatically create instability in the Territories.

The financial institutions now available to residents of the Territories provide a basic, though fragmented, payments system within the Territories, with Israel, and, to a certain extent, between Jordan and the West Bank. But as a result of the situation in the Occupied Territories, those banks that now exist have been little used except as places to store funds safely. Vigorous lending has not occurred: flows of credit from the financial institutions to the business sector and local residents are remarkably small, even though the saving rate is high. There can be no doubt that the development of a more effective financial system would significantly increase the level of non-residential investment and might also further increase the saving rate.

Current economic and political uncertainties in the Occupied Territories must have hindered the development of a wide range of insurance functions. Without a stable system of comprehensible economic rules and regulations governing the financial system, it is impossible to design an insurance system that would be satisfactory to both the user and the provider. Insurance can deal with risks but not with uncertainty about the nature and stability of the financial system itself. Thus the provision of insurance will likely grow when a peace agreement begins to operate.

The task of this report is to make proposals that would enhance the ability of the financial system in the Occupied Territories to fulfill the basic financial system functions—a stable monetary framework, an efficient payments system, an effective system of financial intermediation, and efficient risk-sharing—during the transition period, and in a way that does not preclude relevant possibilities after the transition period. We also view the transition period as a time for institution building, in which new institutions can be set up and can learn to operate. It is thus a period of training for the individuals who will run governmental and private institutions during the transition period and beyond.

The Starting Point

Economic development in the Occupied Territories requires improvements in the system of financial intermediation. As a starting point for our recommendations, we make the following assumptions about the nature of the peace agreements with respect to monetary matters in the West Bank and Gaza:

• The shekel and the dinar will remain legal tender on the West Bank, but the shekel will be augmented by the dinar in Gaza during the transition period;

• No new currency will be introduced during the early stages of the transition;

• A Palestinian Interim Monetary and Financial Authority (PIMFA) will be set up to pursue the goals of financial sector development in the Occupied Territories.

• The central banks of Jordan and Israel will continue to be involved in supervising banks chartered by them, and will be represented on the board of the PIMFA.

We also recommend that the PIMFA should not impose capital controls on flows into and out of the West Bank and Gaza. To grow rapidly, the West Bank and Gaza must attract capital from abroad. To do that, it must be easy for capital to leave the region. The ability to get out is always a central ingredient of any decision to go in.

Given the number of people who live in the West Bank and in Gaza but who work in Israel, one has to envision an open flow of capital and currencies between the two areas. A peace agreement would eventually result in a similar flow of people, and hence capital and currencies, among Jordan, the Palestinian entity, and Israel. Thus one has to envision a set of open, closely intertwined, economies rather than of separate, closed, economies.

Such relations would pose difficulties for Israeli capital controls. While Israeli citizens could be prohibited from dealing with Jordanian and Palestinian banks, these controls would surely be porous and eventually ineffective.

We see three possible ways for Israel to react to the need for open capital movements in the West Bank and Gaza. One is to attempt to control capital flows between Israel and the West Bank and Gaza, and to respond by relaxing controls as the controls themselves are gradually eroded. This approach would limit economic relations between Israel and the West Bank and Gaza, a result that would harm both parties. The second approach would be to allow free capital movements to the West Bank and Gaza, while seeking to maintain controls over capital flows to the rest of the world. This approach would be ineffective, since it would take very little time for the private sector to exploit the inconsistency between Israeli capital controls and West Bank-Gaza freedom for capital to flow to the rest of the world. The third possibility—which we favor—is for Israel to accelerate the general decontrol of capital movements that it has undertaken in the last eight years.

Tasks of the Palestinian Interim Monetary and Financial Authority (PIMFA)

The primary mission of the PIMFA will be to help improve the financial system in the Territories, and thereby contribute to their economic development. A separate agency is needed both because some of its tasks, such as bank supervision, require specialized knowledge, and to ensure that this important responsibility is firmly lodged with a single institution.

The initial responsibilities of the PIMFA would be as set out in Table 6.2. Depending on the overall progress of the transition process, the PIMFA could begin to exercise more functions as the transition proceeds.

As the transition gets under way, it is likely both that existing banks will want to set up new branches in the West Bank and Gaza and that new banks will want to open. PIMFA should be the chartering authority for the new banks and the regulatory authority that grants permission for the opening of new branches. It should also work in conjunction with the Israeli and Jordanian central banks in exercising regulation over the existing banks. Eventually these responsibilities could be transferred solely to it.

Table 6.2
Functions of the Palestinian Interim Monetary and Financial Authority (PIMFA)

---

1. Chartering, supervision and regulation of new banks as well as supervision and regulation of existing commercial banks in the Territories (in coordination with the central banks of Israel and Jordan).

2. Chartering and supervision of non-bank financial intermediaries (coordinated with the regulatory authorities of Jordan and Israel).

3. Collection and publication of data on the financial system; advising the PIMFA on macro-economic policy.

4. Shared responsibility for the creation and operation of necessary public sector financial institutions and intermediaries, such as a development bank (if any such institutions are created.)

Since, during the transition process, both existing and new banks will be issuing either shekel or dinar deposits, and since the adverse consequences of weak banking regulation and performance would be visited eventually on the central bank that issues the currency in which the adversely affected accounts are denominated, both the Bank of Israel and the Central Bank of Jordan will have to participate in the regulatory process. Further, since the Bank of Israel and the Central Bank of Jordan are both already regulating banks in the Territories, it should be possible for them to collaborate by working with PIMFA. In this way the regulatory and supervisory experience of the two central banks could be transferred to the staff of the PIMFA.

PIMFA should definitely consider the opening of more banks in the Occupied Territories as a major operational goal, but must simultaneously ensure that capital and other requirements are satisfied. It would make good sense for PIMFA to adhere to the Basle capital standards. Reserve requirements and other ratios should generally be the same as those in the country in whose currency an account is denominated.

Neither Israel nor Jordan has a formal system of deposit insurance, and PIMFA is unlikely to be able to provide such insurance for deposits denominated in either shekels or dinars. The absence of deposit insurance makes it absolutely crucial that PIMFA exercise vigilant supervision over the banking system.

In many countries, specialized private institutions finance particular types of activity—for instance, building societies finance home purchases. In other countries, universal banks, which essentially provide all financial services, dominate the financial system. Given the small size of the economy of the Occupied Territories, a system with *universal banks* might be preferable.

A universal bank provides a very broad range of financial services beyond the normal deposit taking, check clearing, loans, and foreign exchange operations. In addition to the above services, a universal bank may: lend for a broad range of purposes, including housing finance; serve as an investment bank, extending long-term financing to firms, or sometimes taking an equity position; provide brokerage services; and operate mutual funds.

The distinction between narrow and universal banking is closely related to the difference between the British-United States banking tradition and the Continental-Japanese tradition. Continental banks act also as investment banks, and frequently play an important role in the firms with which they have relationships, typically by having representatives on the board of directors. Israel has universal banks, as does Jordan and most Arab countries. The active involvement of the banks in monitoring firms has been seen as an advantage, and is one route through which specialized business expertise can be applied to a broad range of firms. The major disadvantage of the continental tradition is that it may tie banks too closely to firms, leading the banks to continue lending in the hope of recovering their initial investments, and that it may give the banks too much power.[6]

Even with universal banking, other financial institutions, such as insurance companies and pension funds, venture capital providers, and perhaps savings and loan associations, will be needed in the Occupied Territories. PIMFA should serve as the regulatory and licensing authority for these institutions. Representatives of the regulatory authorities for these types of

---

6. There is currently a major controversy in Israel over the question of whether the banks control too much of the economy. Critics of the current system argue that the banks should be broken up to enhance competition; some, but not the essence, of their suggestions have been embodied in recent legislation.

institutions in Israel and Jordan should be members of the PIMFA regulatory committee for the relevant institutions.

At some point, a stock exchange may be set up in the Occupied Territories. Stock exchanges are sometimes indepen-dent, self-regulating corporations, but, at the same time, they need to operate within a regulatory framework that both ensures that the public is provided with information needed to evaluate company performance and that keeps speculative behavior in the market under control. If there is a move to set up a stock exchange, PIMFA should take the lead in organizing the regulatory framework for its operation—without necessari-ly itself taking charge of day-to-day regulation.

Since PIMFA will receive balance sheet information from all financial institutions in the Territories, it should also be respon-sible for collecting and publishing data on the financial system. The range of information typically published in industrialized countries can be discerned from the *Bulletins* of any of the major central banks, such as the Bundesbank, Federal Reserve Bank or the Bank of England, or from the publications of the Central Bank of Jordan or the Bank of Israel. PIMFA would publish a much smaller amount of information, perhaps in a quarterly. It might at the same time publish a commentary on recent eco-nomic developments in the West Bank and Gaza, in a publica-tion similar to the Bank of Israel's *Recent Economic Developments*. For these purposes, PIMFA would need a Research Department for data collection and analysis.

Many developing countries have set up public-sector devel-opment banks to finance either development projects or special sectors of the economy. For instance, a development bank may provide special financing for agricultural sector investments, or it may finance infrastructure projects with the assistance of external aid. The overall record of such banks is mixed, with several down sides: loan allocations are often more dependent on political than economic considerations; poor repayment records; and, in some instances, corruption. If it is decided to set up a development bank to fill some perceived gap in the financial system—a move we do not recommend, it will be important to ensure that its management and Board of Directors operate according to commercial principles.

Many countries have in the past operated postal savings systems, and many continue to do so. In this system, individuals hold accounts in savings banks set up within post offices. The postal savings bank typically invests all its assets in government bonds and remits the interest to depositors. Since its deposits are fully covered by government bonds, they are effectively insured. The postal savings system in Japan remains the largest deposit-taking institution in the country, and it deploys its assets in directions favored by the government. Postal savings systems in Europe and elsewhere also operate a highly efficient giro payments system, whose scope is as wide as that of the postal system.

Whether the interim government will be able to set up a postal savings system depends, obviously, on whether it will operate the postal system in the West Bank and Gaza during the transition. The benefits of setting up a postal savings system are that it provides a convenient and widely accessible vehicle for individual saving, that it may provide a large flow of resources to the government, and that it makes it possible to set up an efficient domestic payments system. The main disadvantage is that the system competes, often unfairly, with private-sector deposit-taking institutions.

Given that neither Israel nor Jordan has a system of deposit insurance and that confidence needs to be reinstated in the banking system after a period in which bank accounts have not been considered safe because of fears of military intervention, a system of postal savings accounts might make a lot of sense during the transition to a system in which private banks play their usual pivotal role.

Organization of the PIMFA

The PIMFA would be governed by a board of directors headed by a chairman appointed by the interim government, and would include representatives of the central banks of Israel and Jordan. The board should include representatives of the private sector in the Territories, but should be dominated by professionals.

One possible arrangement is for the board to consist of the chairman, the CEO of the development bank (if such a bank is ever established), representatives of the private banks and the chambers of commerce (or other members of the private sector active in industry and commerce) in the West Bank and Gaza respectively, a representative from each of the central banks of Jordan and Israel, and the three members of PIMFA's senior management. The non-private sector members of the board should have the power to approve the representatives chosen by the private sector. The agreement of the representatives of the Banks of Israel or Jordan would, for some initial period, be needed for any decisions involving institutions operating in their currency.

Internally, the PIMFA would be run by a managing board, consisting of the chairman and heads of the main departments. These departments would include:

• a banking department, responsible for chartering and supervision of banks;

• a non-bank financial institutions department;

• an external economic relations department, responsible for relations with the neighboring central banks, and with operations undertaken by non-Palestinian banks in the Territories;

• a research and advisory department.

Decisions of the managing board would be subject to review by the board of directors.

The Future

It is important to regard the transition process itself as a period of potential change. The powers of the PIMFA should evolve over time. At the beginning it would be natural that the representatives of the central banks of Jordan and Israel would play a major role, seeking both to ensure that operations of the PIMFA do not create difficulties for them and to help to build up the expertise of the staff of the PIMFA—which should also receive assistance from the IMF and from other countries. As the PIMFA gained experience, it would take on more and more responsibility.

Similarly, as more banks are opened, and as banking develops in the West Bank and Gaza, PIMFA will automatically be responsible for a growing share of the financial intermediaries in the West Bank and Gaza.

Looking beyond the transition period, it is possible that the successor institution would want to introduce an independent currency. It would be an easy transition from the arrangements of the PIMFA to a Currency Board, in which the currency is backed fully by foreign assets, to, eventually, a more fiduciary currency.

7 The Management of Foreign Aid to the West Bank and Gaza: Goals and Organization

Dwight Perkins, *Chair;* Avishay Braverman,
Hind Salman, Munther A. Share'

Management of foreign aid is not a separate subject from the general issue of the management of the economy of the West Bank and Gaza. Indeed, for the immediate future foreign financial assistance is likely to be the principal source of funds for public investment, and may also be a source of funding for private investment and public current expenditures. In addition, foreign technical assistance could make an important contribution to the design of economic institutions and the management of the economy during the interim period and later. Foreign assistance therefore has the potential to play a central role in the economic development of the West Bank and Gaza once these territories gain control over their economic and social affairs.

The Organization of Foreign Aid

The task of setting development priorities belong in the hands of the most senior economic managers of the self-governing authority, working closely with the duly constituted political leadership. Given the likely importance of foreign aid to the economy, and the multiplicity of likely aid donors and agencies, high priority will have to be given to the management of aid.

The tasks of aid management include:

• The preparation of aid requests, based on the priorities of the governing authority, determined in consultation with all the economic ministries;

• Negotiation of aid agreements with donors;

• Overall management of the financing and the execution of projects;

• The coordination of the activities of the donors, to ensure that they do not operate at cross purposes with each other and with the development goals of the interim self-government.

All these functions fall under the broad heading of liaison between Palestinian economic decision-makers and the officials of the different aid agencies. We describe these activities as aid coordination, though they should be understood as going well beyond coordination. The aid coordination function should be located in whichever body has the responsibility for setting and implementing economic priorities.

In Chapter 4, we proposed that the foreign aid coordination function be lodged in the Department of Finance. An alternative set-up is to have the aid agency in the Department of Development, with aid responsibilities then coordinated with the Department of Finance. We prefer the former arrangement.

Whatever the public sector structure, the aid coordination agency must be integrated with the agency responsible for the overall management of economic policy. Otherwise there are in effect two policy and planning agencies, one coordinating policy and projects financed by aid, and the other coordinating policy and projects financed with domestic revenues. To be effective a policy and planning agency must have control over the major development resources available. Otherwise it becomes a decorative body that draws up plans to which no one pays any attention.

Wherever the aid coordinating body is located, it needs to carry out the basic functions specified above. An important part of the task is quite mechanical. Aid agencies have various procedures that must be followed before a grant is made. Most aid agencies only adjust country priorities once every two years or longer and, to influence these priorities, one must be prepared to make one's case at these specific times. One of the aid coordinator's roles is to keep track of all of these procedures and timetables and to advise policy makers as to what they need to do and when they need to do it.

At a more substantive level aid coordinators need to understand the thinking of the various aid agencies and their resident representatives. They also need to know the priorities of their own leaders. The coordinator's role is then to try to bring these different viewpoints closer together so that decisions in support of development can be made.

Given that aid is already flowing to Palestinians in the West Bank and Gaza, consideration should be given to setting up an aid coordination agency even before the functional equivalent of a planning board or a ministry of finance is established. Alternatively one could create a policy and planning board immediately, recognizing that its major immediate function will be to coordinate external assistance. This policy and planning board and/or aid coordinating agency would then have to be integrated with other economic agencies set up as the self-governing authority comes into existence.

Aid Objectives and Instruments

The ultimate objective of foreign assistance to the West Bank and Gaza will be to create the conditions for vibrant, largely private sector-led, economic development. But in the current state of the economy of the Occupied Territories, where the economic development of the Palestinians has not been a goal of policy, there will be a need also for a strong public sector involvement in economic development and infrastructure investment. Where the line between public and private sector activities should be drawn will depend on specific conditions in the individual sectors, but it is likely that the interim self-government will have to take charge of some projects that would, in other circumstances, be handled privately.

International agreement on the importance of peace in the Middle East and the development of the Palestinian entity should make foreign governments and international organizations willing to provide financial aid to the self-governing authority, on a scale that is significant relative to the size of the economy.[1] Indeed, as we detail below, the volume of aid to the Palestinians is already significant.

The role of foreign aid will therefore be large and diverse, particularly in the early years while a self-governing structure is being created and the private sector is being revitalized. Several different types of aid will be needed:

Project Aid

Aid designated to support specific projects will be a major feature of assistance to the West Bank and Gaza for the indefinite future. Donors have their own priorities and they like to see their aid go to those priorities even if, in practice, much aid is fungible (aid given for one purpose frees up funds from other sources to be used for other purposes). Project aid takes many forms. The priority areas for West Bank and Gaza project assistance include:

---

1. The Palestinians will be helped by the small size of the economy; one of the strong empirical regularities in the aid process is that smaller countries tend to receive larger amounts of aid *per capita* than larger countries at a similar stage of development.

Aid Funds to Support Infrastructure Projects
The funding of public infrastructure projects is a traditional use of foreign assistance. Until major new sources of revenue are generated, foreign aid is likely to be the main source of funding for public infrastructure and other development projects. Initially, there may be a need for aid funds for private sector projects as well. Over time, as the domestic banking system in the West Bank and Gaza develops, and as private external lending becomes available, the need to use aid funds for this purpose will decline or disappear. Until then aid funds can often help generate private funds through co-financing arrangements such as those promoted by the private lending arm of the World Bank, the International Finance Corporation. Aid funds can also be, and frequently are, used to help create new financial institutions whose primary role is to lend to the private sector.

Aid should not be used as a reason for placing a project within the public or private sectors. The primary goal of all development efforts in the West Bank and Gaza should be to create dynamic private sector-led development and all foreign assistance should be consistent with that objective.

Funds to Support Training and Education
Shortages of technical personnel needed to develop both the public and private sectors are bound to emerge as the self-governing authority is established. In some cases existing training/education institutions can be strengthened, in other cases new institutions will have to be created from scratch. While local institutions are being strengthened or built, foreign project aid will be a major source of funds for sending people abroad for training. In other cases the demand for specific skills will not be sufficient to justify establishing training institutions in the West Bank or Gaza and all training/education will be obtained by sending students abroad.

Funds to Support Foreign Technical Assistance
While people are being trained, many public and private institutions will want to strengthen their staffing by the hiring of expatriates to fill gaps and to provide on the job training. This practice is widespread in developing countries, including those of Eastern Europe and the former Soviet Union. Aid funds could also be used to attract back Palestinians with special skills.[2] Aid funds for these two kinds of external technical assistance are likely to be needed for the first five to ten years after the creation of authority for economic management in the Territories.

Aid Funds to Support Welfare Programs for Low Income People
Inevitably, the development process in the West Bank and Gaza will leave some people behind, with insufficient resources to ensure access to minimal levels of basic needs (food, housing, health and education). Aid agencies have typically helped fund efforts to assist the poor, often working through non-governmental organizations (NGOs) of various kinds as well as through governments. There will clearly continue to be a role for this kind of aid in the West Bank and Gaza for some years into the future.

General Program Aid

Program aid is general non-project financing, to fund the public sector budget, and for balance of payments support. It is quite likely that the revenues of the self-governing authority from taxation and other sources in the West Bank and Gaza, and from agreed transfers from the Israeli government, will fall short of projected expenditures, at least in the early years. Since the self-

---

2. The Korean Institute of Science and Technology and the Korean Development Institute, both set up with foreign assistance, had as their primary objective attracting back Koreans trained and employed abroad. Both are regarded as successful institutions.

governing authority will not have access to the printing press, any shortfall of revenues will have to be covered by borrowing and by foreign assistance. Borrowing may be from local sources, or from abroad, particularly from bilateral and multilateral development agencies. In addition, friendly governments may provide grants to the self-governing authority.

Foreign aid may be needed as well to close any balance of payments financing gap that emerges once the development plans of the self-governing authority have been specified. The international agencies, the IMF and the World Bank, routinely calculate balance of payments financing gaps or requirements in their discussions of the economic plans of member countries. We discuss below the question of how and whether the self-governing authority will be able to gain access to the technical assistance of the international agencies. In any case, such calculations are relatively simple, and would emerge as part of the overall economic plans of the self-governing authority.

While it is natural to calculate spending plans on the basis of need, all economic units have to tailor their spending plans to available resources. If domestic and foreign revenue sources are insufficient to finance needed spending, the spending plans will have to be adjusted.

In the early years, foreign assistance may be used to finance recurrent as well as capital spending by the public sector. As the self-governing authority establishes its fiscal system, the use of foreign assistance to support recurrent expenditures should be phased out.

Regional Projects

Foreign aid can play an essential role in the development of regional projects that involve several countries in the region. Given the small size of many states in the region and the vital role of such joint resources as water and transport facilities, regional infrastructure projects will be essential if these resources are to be used efficiently. Regional projects will also be important vehicles through which the people in the region can learn to work together for constructive ends. External aid funding will often be an essential incentive to bring such projects into being.

We return to the subject of regional projects and cooperation below.

Existing Uses of Foreign Aid and the Role of NGOs

Current foreign aid funds going to the West Bank and Gaza bear little relation to the broad range of objectives just listed. Because of the current political situation, there is neither program aid nor project aid for transportation and other infrastructure. But the composition of even the remaining project aid is unusual.

A list of projects currently supported by aid funds is presented in Appendix A. The amount of aid currently allocated to the West Bank and Gaza is not small. UNRWA provides about $120 million per annum and the aggregate for the West Bank and Gaza may be about $200 million per annum.

Projects now underway have received aid commitments of US $202 million, although many of these are multi-year projects. Of this total 42 percent went to the health sector. Education received nearly 18 percent, with the remaining 40 percent being allocated to all other development objectives. Most of these funds were routed through Palestinian and donor NGOs and understandably reflected what the NGOs were best able to do. Donors interested in providing direct support to the people of the West Bank and Gaza had few other aid disbursing vehicles at their disposal.

The bulk of the aid that went to economic development projects was concentrated on a only a handful of projects. For example, of the US $22 million allocated to the development of industry, US $10.6 million, or 48 percent, went to a single fruit processing plant in Gaza. This project may well be an excellent one (we are not in a position to judge), but clearly a single fruit processing plant does not constitute an effective industrial development program for a population of close to two million.

Foreign assistance funds available to the West Bank and Gaza in the future are likely to be much larger than those currently available. Whether these funds should be concentrated on a few specific projects or on more general program aid is a judgment that will have to be made by the aid planning authorities of the West Bank and Gaza in conjunction with the aid donors, in the context of the general development priorities set by the self-governing authority. Most likely aid will be used for both program and project purposes. It is clearly desirable that a much larger share of aid go to support general development objectives than at present. These objectives will include but go well beyond health and welfare goals; while health expenditures could rise and/or change in composition, it is certain that general economic development aid will have to increase.

NGOs will continue to be recipients of aid in the future and they will continue in many cases to operate independently of the economic planners and aid coordinators in the West Bank and Gaza. NGOs often have advantages over government agencies when it comes to certain kinds of welfare interventions, particularly in small, local projects. But even in the welfare area, NGOs seldom have the capacity, even collectively, to deal with the welfare needs of an entire population. And NGOs are clearly not appropriate recipients for balance of payment support and other program aid or for infrastructure project aid, and the like.

The existing aid structure developed during a period of occupation, and it is therefore inadequate to the accomplishment of the broad economic tasks that will face the self-governing authority. A new aid coordination agency should not, however, aim to supplant the NGOs. Instead it should recognize their ability to work closely with local residents, and seek to coordinate NGO efforts to eliminate duplication and conflict.

The Role of External Organizations

Technical Assistance

The primary responsibility for setting economic and social priorities in the use of foreign assistance may rest on a West Bank and Gaza foreign aid agency within a Department of Finance. However, while this agency is being set up and probably for several years thereafter, it is unlikely to have the experience and skills required for all the tasks it faces. Some of this experience gap can be filled by technical assistance, through small teams of individuals working on contract with the West Bank and Gaza economics departments and especially the foreign aid agency. These teams or individuals would be responsible to the Palestinians running the agency, not to the donors providing the funds to make this assistance possible. In addition, some Palestinians who have gained experience abroad, for instance in international agencies, are likely to be available to aid the development effort.

Technical assistance in setting up the institutions of economic management would best be provided by the international agencies most experienced at doing so. For instance, the IMF has extensive international experience in the design of fiscal systems and central banks; the World Bank has assisted in the reform and design of financial systems all over the world. The EC has also been active in providing technical assistance in Eastern Europe and the former Soviet Union.

The Role of the IFIs

More generally, there is a growing consensus that a major financial institution should be involved in the economic development of the West Bank and Gaza, and of the entire Middle East, in conjunction with the peace process. What is needed for the Territories is an institution which will 1) make an appropriate assessment for the donors, and in conjunction with the Palestinian foreign aid coordination agency, of the development needs and priorities within the West Bank and Gaza; 2) set up a framework to coordinate donor assistance, in conjunction with the Palestinian foreign aid agency; 3) help manage general and project aid to the West Bank and Gaza; and 4) provide technical assistance to the self-governing authority. In addition to coordinating assistance from donors, the agency might, if legal conditions permitted, also lend directly to the self-governing authority.

The leading international financial institution, the World Bank, is the natural and appropriate institution to take on these responsibilities. It has vast experience in dealing fairly with conflicting parties. It has begun to play an active role in the multilateral talks between Israel and the Arab countries and is prepared to continue in that role as long as it is desired by all sides. Further, the World Bank is capable of mobilizing the best expertise both from the region and around the world.

As long as the self-governing authority lacks sovereignty, it cannot become a regular member of the Bretton Woods institutions. However, it should not be beyond the abilities of the international community to enable the international financial institutions (IFIs) to provide technical assistance to the West Bank and Gaza, and to coordinate financial assistance from other donors. For instance, special trust funds could be set up to finance technical assistance, and to pay the costs of World Bank (and where appropriate, IMF) staff involved in the planning and coordination of the overall aid effort.

A Regional Bank

What is needed for the development of the Middle East is an agency which will focus on regional projects, and on regional coordination and cooperation in economic management. Such an agency would serve as the forum for the discussion and solution of problems of mutual interest, and in so doing contribute to expanding cooperation within the region.

While the World Bank could take the lead in setting up regional projects, there is a strong case for creating a regional development bank. This bank, which might be called the Middle Eastern Bank for Cooperation and Development, would have the task of developing regional projects and fostering regional cooperation. The creation of a new regional bank, led by distinguished and experienced professionals including Israelis and Arabs, could provide a major signal of a new spirit of cooperation and creativity in the region. Because it would emphasize and encourage functional cooperation among the residents of the countries of the region, such a Bank would have a different role and rationale than the World Bank. There is currently interest and discussion of this matter.

The MEBCD could start out small, concentrating at first on economic cooperation among Jordan, the West Bank and Gaza, and Israel. Its membership would include countries of the Middle East and elsewhere that support the peace process. While the MEBCD would start out financing regional projects relevant to the economies of Israel, Jordan, and the West Bank and Gaza, it would gradually broaden its activities to include regional projects involving other Middle Eastern countries.

Such a regional bank would have a regular development banking function. It would borrow in international capital markets and lend at market rates to projects likely to earn market rates of return. It could also have special funds lent on more concessional terms much like the International Development Association of the World Bank. By channeling funds through this regional bank, donors would have more confidence that the funds would be well used than would be the case with many bilateral projects.

The MEBCD would be financed through capital contributions by member countries. Because a major goal of the new bank would be to enable people from different parts of the region to learn to live together, there should be a preference for staffing the bank with residents of the region. Initially the largest contributions to the bank might come from outside the region, but gradually the majority of shares and hence membership on the board would be owned by countries within the region. Regional ownership and control, acquired with all deliberate speed, is the answer to the fear that such a regional bank would become a vehicle for the imposition of control over the local economies from outside the region.

Getting Started

There is little chance that a new regional bank can be set up soon enough to have an impact on the development of the West Bank and Gaza, and the region, within a year. Accordingly, the World Bank or some other institution should be encouraged by all parties to begin to help develop economic programs for the Territories. This would involve: 1) preparation of an economic development plan for the West Bank and Gaza, including the establishment of trust funds through which projects and technical assistance for the West Bank and Gaza could be financed;

and 2) the assessment of major projects that involve several countries, perhaps in conjunction with the multilateral negotiations. The World Bank or other institution could also begin to coordinate policy and act as a clearinghouse for the various aid organizations currently active in the region, while the West Bank and Gaza policy and planning agency is being set up.

We further recommend that work begin on setting up the MEBCD. Although the international community has not been receptive to the establishment of yet another international development bank, we believe that the focus of this bank—on cooperation within the region—and its organization, with residents of the region playing an important role, makes it different from the standard regional bank. As an organization set up to foster practical cooperation among the residents of the region, the MEBCD could make an important contribution to a durable peace.

A Think-Tank

Whether or not a new regional bank is formed soon, there is also a role for a think-tank with experts from both inside and outside the West Bank and Gaza to provide counsel in the development of the economic plans for the area in general and the Territories in particular. Such a think-tank would be led from the outset by development specialists from the West Bank and Gaza, but its staff could include expatriate specialists particularly in the early years. Such a think-tank would be primarily responsible for providing in-depth analysis and a long term perspective to the policy and planning efforts of those managing aid and development expenditures on a daily basis. This think-tank would complement, not compete with, the more regional perspective of analysts in the proposed regional bank.

Appendix A: Aid to the West Bank and Gaza, 1992

This Appendix lists aid provided to the West Bank and Gaza by private voluntary organizations (PVOs), sometimes referred to as Non-Governmental Organizations (NGOs), The data were derived from those in "Assistance to the Occupied Palestinian Territories—1992; Compendium of Ongoing and Planned Projects," compiled by the United Nations Development Program and released in April 1992 in Jerusalem.

The Compendium contains projects which were under implementation in 1992 and planned for 1992. Although the budgets of the projects often cover different durations, the total figures provide a general indication of overall priorities adopted by the donors. Health is the most favored sector and has 41.89% of the budget; it is followed by Education, Industry and Agriculture with 17.62%, 10.89% and 8.58% of the budget, respectively. All other percentages are shown under the classification of each of the 15 sectors that follow.

Contributions by donor countries to United Nations agencies for specific projects have been included, but not their contributions to the United Nations agencies' regular budgets for relief purposes (which started in 1948).

Assistance to the Occupied Territories in the last few years has been given by 66 different donors and implementing agencies. There has been little coordination among them, especially since the start of the Intifada. The data in this Appendix was compiled by the UNDP *after* the grants or loans were given.

The sector classifications and budgets for each project follow. For the first three sectors all the donors and the implementing agencies or organizations are listed, to present a picture of how many are in the field. The rest of the classifications do not have the names of the donors or implementing agency or organization. Acronyms for the 28 implementing agencies (out of a total of 66 agencies active in the West Bank and Gaza) of projects described in this Appendix are provided at the end of the Appendix.

Sector Classifications

1. General Development
Issues, Policy and Planning $1,382,117 (0.68%)

• Development strategies,
policies and planning
• General statistics
• Public administration

Donors: *Implementing Agency/Organization:*
Canada   Canada Fund/Local NGOs
U.K.   British Consulate Jerusalem
E.E.C.   Market Experts Consultants

2. Natural Resources $7,731,390 (3.82%)

• Biological resources
• Cartography
• Energy
• Land and Water
• Mineral resources

Donors: *Implementing Agency/Organization:*
Japan   UNDP
Netherlands   IWACO, ICC/ICCO
U.K.   OXFAM, Newcastle University
E.E.C.   Jerusalem Water Authority
UNDP   UNDP
USAID   SCF, CDP, CRS

3. Agriculture, Forestry
and Fisheries $17,352,938 (8.58%)

• Agricultural development
support services
• Crops
• Fisheries
• Forestry
• Livestock

Donors: *Implementing Agency/Organization*
Australia   APHEDA
Austria   SAAR
Canada   Canada Fund/Local organizations

Finland	PARC
France	French Consulate
Italy	COCIS/C.I.S.S., COCIS/Mani-Tese, Progetto Sviluppo/CGIL
Japan	UNDP
Netherlands	Arab Thought Forum/NOVIB, PARC Gaza/NOVIB, Hebron University
Norway	Palestine Groups in Norway
Spain	TDC, CPU Gaza, ADCC, PARC, EDG, Latin Patriarchate/Dev. Office
Sweden	SOIR/PARC
U.K.	OXFAM, UNAIS, Christian Aid/PARC, Action Around Bethlehem/BASPH
E.E.C.	ADCC, ARDG Jerusalem, OXFAM, EDG, ADS, Arab Fund/Econ. & Soc. Dev., Crocevia, C. Int. Hautes Etudes Agro., Bank of Palestine Gaza, Welfare Association
UNDP	UNDP
USAID	CDP, SCF, ANERA, CRS

4. Industry $22,037, 786 (10.89%)

• Industrial development support services
• Manufacturing industries
• Other service industries
• Tourism and related services

Of the total, the following amounts were spent on the Citrus Processing Plant in Gaza:

Donors:	*Implementing Agency/Organization:*	
Italy	UNDP	
1990	Citrus Processing Plant in Gaza Strip	$9,597,000
UNDP	UNDP	
1990	Establishment of Citrus Processing Plant in Gaza Strip	$1,000,000
Total		$10,597,000

This means that 48% of the budget for industry was devoted to one project.

5. Trade and
Development Finance $727,770 (0.36%)

• Development finance and monetary problems
• Global trade policies

- Trade in commodities
- Trade in manufactures
- Trade promotion and trade in services

6. Population $295,828 (0.15%)

- Family planning
- Population dynamics

7. Housing and Infrastructure $4,900,973 (2.42%)

8. Health $84,689,792 (41.89%)

- Comprehensive health services
- Disease prevention and control
- Environmental health

Consider also the amount of money spent on the Sewage Project for Bethlehem/Beit Sahur/Beit Jala;

Donors:	Implementing Agency/Organization:	
Germany	GTZ	
1990	Bethlehem/Beit Sahur/Beit Jala	
	Sewage Project	$8,536,585
Italy	UNDP/Italian Cooperation/DGCS	
1990	Bethlehem/Beit Sahur/Beit Jala	
	Sewage Project	$6,600,000
Total		**$15,136,585**

This implies that $15,136,585 / $84,689,792 = 18%$ of the entire (and quite large) aid project for health went for one project.

9. Education $35,637,415 (17.62%)

- Educational facilities and technology
- Educational policy and planning
- Educational systems
- Non-formal education

10. Employment   no figures supplied

- Conditions of employment
- Employment promotion and planning
- Industrial relations
- Skills development

11. Humanitarian Aid and Relief $11,885,819 (5.89%)

- Disaster, relief preparedness and prevention
- Protection of and assistance to refugees and displaced persons
- Special humanitarian operations

12. Social Conditions and Equity	$ 6,933,517 (3.44%)

- Advancement of women
- Disadvantaged groups
- Human rights
- Prevention of crime and drug abuse
- Social sciences
- Welfare and social security

13. Culture	$1,904,798 (0.94%)

- Communication and mass media
- Cultural preservations and development
- Protection of authors and performers

14. Science and Technology	$1,172,620 (0.58%)

- Development and transfer of technology
- Meteorology
- Oceanography
- Promotion of Science

15. Multisectoral	$5,539,089 (2.74%)

Grand Total	**$202,191,852 (100%)**

Additional Foreign Credit and Aid
The following foreign credit and aid was given after the UNDP Compendium on aid was published: UNRWA gave 4 new loans amounting to $131,000 for production enterprises in the Gaza Strip. The loans were distributed as follows:

	$US
Biscuit Factory in Al-Durj	35,000
Neon Bulbs Factory	10,000
Handbags in Breij Camp	35,000
Meat Products Factory in Maghazi Camp	51,000
Total	**$131,000**

(Al-Quds, 17/5/1992, page 2)

The EEC will contribute $16.7 million to build a hospital with 232 beds in Khan Yunis in the Gaza Strip. Construction will start in 1993 and end in 1995.

(Al-Quds, 18/6/1992, page 3)

The EEC has announced that it will contribute US $80 million which will be spent on housing projects, hospitals and businesses.

(Al-Quds, 15/7/1992, page 2)

List of Acronyms Used

The acronyms of the implementing agencies are provided in Annex III of the UNDP Compendium and they total 66 in number. Here only the 28 used above are listed.

ADCC	Arab Development and Credit Company
ADS	Arab Development Society
ANERA	American Near East Refugee Aid
APHEDA	Australian People for Health, Education and Development Abroad
ARDG	Applied Research Development Group
BASPH	Bethlehem Arab Society for Physically Handicapped
CDP	Cooperative Development Project
CISS	Cooperazione Internazionale SUD-SUD
COCIS	Coordinamento delle Organizzazioni non Governative per la Cooperazione Internazionale allo Sviluppo. Italian NGOs for International Development Cooperation
CPU	Citrus Producers Union
CRS	Catholic Relief Services
DGCS	Direzione Generale Per la Cooperazione allo Sviluppo. Department for Development Cooperation
EDG	Economic Development Group
EEC	Economic European Community
GTZ	Deutsche Gesellschaft für Technische Zusammenarbeit. German Association for Technical Cooperation.
ICC	International Christian Committee
ICCO	International Coordination Committee for Development Projects
IWACO	Consultants for Water and Environment
NOVIB	Netherlands Organization for International Assistance
OXFAM	Oxford Committee for Famine Relief
PARC	Palestinian Agricultural Relief Committee
SAAR	Society for Austro-Arab Relations
SCF	Save the Children Federation
SOIR	Swedish Organization for Individual Relief
TDC	Technical Development Corporation
UNAIS	United Nations Association for International Service
UNDP	United Nations Development Programme
USAID	United States Agency for International Development

8   The Way Ahead

Stanley Fischer, *Steering Committee Co-Chair*

The recommendations made in this report point the way to a future in which Palestinians, Jordanians, and Israelis can enjoy free and open economic relations conducive to their economic development and long term prosperity.

Most of the recommendations will begin to be translated into practice when peace agreements are reached among the Palestinians and Israel, Israel and Jordan, and Israel and other countries in the Middle East. Those agreements will specify the nature of the Palestinian interim self-governing authority and its powers, including "economic sovereignty." Those agreements will be the basis for the framework in which economic relations among the three economies will be conducted.

But there is no need to wait until the final peace agreements to begin working on the economic approach to peace. Progress toward peace could be accelerated by taking immediate action that anticipate the eventual agreement. Specifically:

1. The Israeli, Jordanian and Palestinian delegations should announce an agreement on the general principles that will guide their economic relations of free and open trade in a market-dominated policy environment.

2. The Israelis and Palestinians should announce an agreement on the principle that the Palestinian interim self-governing

authority will have economic sovereignty over the West Bank and Gaza within the framework to be reached in the final agreements.

3. The parties should appoint teams of experts, possibly assisted by external experts, to:

a. develop a plan for the implementation of free trade agreements between Israel and the West Bank and Gaza; between the West Bank and Gaza and Jordan; and between Jordan and Israel; leading to a free trade area among the three economies, and perhaps extending to other countries in the region;

b. develop plans for regional projects in the area of transportation, tourism, energy, and water;

c. develop plans for a regional bank for development and economic cooperation;

d. prepare proposals for tax harmonization and revenue recovery between Israel and the West Bank and Gaza;

e. develop a plan for the long term development of the Palestinian economy, including detailed plans for infrastructure investment and estimates of its cost;

f. prepare estimates of the likely budgeting and balance of payments financing needs of the Palestinian economy (this will require the preparation of a draft budget as well as balance of payments projections);

g. consider the potential structure and role of a foreign aid coordination agency within the interim self-governing authority;

h. develop plans for a Palestinian interim monetary and financial authority;

i. consider the possibility of setting up an agriculture research institute, and a development policy think-tank.

We have specified actions and studies in areas where the issues are important, and where rapid progress is possible. We therefore recommend that all studies should be completed, with action plans specified, within six months of their being commissioned. They can be commissioned within a month.

It is time to move ahead.